YOU DON'T KNOW
THE HALF OF IT

A A R O N
SLIGHT

THE AUTOBIOGRAPHY

111

YOU DON'T KNOW
THE HALF OF IT

A A R O N
SLIGHT

WITH PAUL OWEN

PHANTOM HOUSE

Paul Owen thanks Glenda MacFarlane for typing out transcripts; Mark Petch for his understanding, Simon Garrett and Julian Ryder for their research, and Joy Owen for all the back massages.

Grant Sheehan of Phantom House Books thanks the following for their input, assistance and encouragement:

Paul Owen, Ian Grant, Andrew Meo, Lauren Robertson, Paul Greenberg, Natalie Gray, David Hedley and Shelley-Maree Cassidy.

Thanks to photographers Roger Lohrer, Miguel Herranz, Andre Kammer, Martin Stewart and Megan Slight.

Cover Concept by Tubbs Wanigasekera (tubbs06@hotmail.com)
Cover photograph of Aaron by Grant Sheehan
Back Cover photo by R. Tagliabue (www.hobnob.it)
Additional cover photoshop work by Peter Muller of DAC Group
Edited by Ian F Grant
Page design & photospread layout by Lauren Robertson
Typesetting by Typeface
Printed in Hong Kong by Toppan Printing Co., (H.K.) Ltd.

First Published in New Zealand in 2001 by Phantom House Books Ltd
P O Box 6385 Marion Square
Wellington
New Zealand
Email: phantomh@actrix.gen.nz
www.phantomhouse.com

ISBN 0-473-07908-9

Acknowledgements

When I began to seriously consider writing this book I put a lot of thought into how I wanted it to read. I wanted to give my readers a good 'story'. A real account of my life, with all its ups and downs. Looking over the end result it now seems a very serious and, at times, rather sad saga. In fact, I feel my life to date has been a very successful one, and definitely one that's given me great happiness and sense of achievement. Certainly it's the story of a career I took seriously and never swayed from. It's about hard work, commitment and success. But it's also been great fun!

I would like to take this opportunity to thank Jonathan Green for the concept. He planted the idea in my head and gave me invaluable ideas during the book's early stages. Grant Sheehan and Phantom House Publishing gave these ideas a home.

My wife Megan made many sacrifices for me to chase my dream, and I couldn't have achieved these goals without her support and understanding.

Paul Owen co-wrote my autobiography, and I am proud of what we've done together. I feel this book gives a true and honest account of my career. This was the most important aspect of the book for me, and I'm grateful for Paul's contribution to achieving it.

AARON SLIGHT
October 2001

I would like to dedicate this book to all the people who touched my heart, helped and guided me along the way. My life will be forever richer for the experiences we shared.

And specially, to my family, who were there from the beginning and will be until the end.

Contents

one

It Was All in My Head

It's Monday 14 February 2000. Valentine's Day. I'm driving a rental car on the Pacific Highway in Sydney, Australia, and I'm wondering if I'm going out of my mind.

I keep one eye shut to stop my double vision, aim for the middle of the lane, but seem to keep running over the cats' eyes the whole time. I'm on my way to see yet another doctor to try to find out just what the hell is wrong with me. But I'm clutching at straws. The doctor I'm going to see specialises in Chronic Fatigue Syndrome, which would explain my tiredness, but not why I can't see straight.

I probably shouldn't be driving at all. I'm normally one of the fastest motorcycle riders in the world with reactions and fitness second to none. I've just completed the 1999 World Superbike Championship for Honda and now I can't even drive down a 3- lane highway without hitting the cats' eyes.

The trip to Australia had started with more testing on the new 1000cc V-twin Honda we're developing for the upcoming 2000 season. In '99 I rode a Honda RC45, which is a 4-cylinder 750. The 2000 season is going to be Honda's first attempt at taking the world title with the 1000cc V-twin engine format permitted by World Superbike rules. Manufacturers have the choice of racing either 750cc fours or 1000cc twins, and this would be the first time Honda attempted to break the Ducati stranglehold on the championship by competing with the Italian manufacturer on equal terms. So we have been doing a lot of testing to try to get this new bike up to speed. Throughout the exhaustive work of testing, I've felt like shit, like I've partied hard the night before when all I did was have an early night. I've been sleeping a lot and that's not like me at all. Up until this point I've just been frustrated that I haven't been as sharp as I usually am and annoyed that this was happening now, especially when there's important work to do. I had spent my entire career struggling against the bigger-engined V-twin Ducatis, which have always had an advantage over the 4 cylinders because of the way the rules are written. The World Superbike Championship is not a battle of equals when it comes to engine design. Of course, the big-bore twins proved my point time and time again by winning almost everything in sight, with Carl Fogarty winning four titles on the big red bikes from Bologna.

The 2000 season, though, would be different. Finally I would have a Twin too and Honda was determined to arrive at the first race with something they could be competitive with straight out of the box. That's why we were doing all this testing, for Honda is acknowledged as the mightiest of motorcycle manufacturers. It sells the most bikes, and has the biggest turnover with all the research and development opportunities that allows. If the new VTR racebike isn't on the pace when the flag drops, the powerful Honda Racing Corporation would experience a serious loss of face. Yet I just can't test the bike the way I want to and the fear I'm letting the team down is a rat gnawing at my guts. That morning I finally reached my breaking point. I'd parked my bike at the beginning of the three-day test and walked away, something I'd never done before, but I just couldn't go on. I had to do something so I headed for another doctor. Whatever I had, it was now getting worse by the minute.

Like I said, I didn't think it was CFS (Chronic Fatigue Syndrome) but people had said maybe it was and maybe it wasn't, so I just didn't know whom to turn to.

I had already been to see an eye specialist, a cardio specialist and another gastro specialist who checks out all your insides. He gave me a bowel examination, which confirmed my sexuality - not that there was much doubt there - followed by a CT scan on my body. So far I've seen more doctors than an operating theatre. But none can confirm what is wrong with me.

To add to the confusion most of them told me how healthy I was. In the cardio test, the doctor said I was only the second person to get through his test without my heart rate maxxing out. In a 22-minute test intended to determine my fitness, I hadn't reached the limits of my physical endurance. I'd had I don't know how many blood tests, passed heaps of stool samples, and been on loads of different ridiculous diets. But nothing seemed to help. I just couldn't keep my concentration and felt really tired all the time. I keep saying to the doctors: "I don't feel sharp. I'm losing my alertness - that sixth sense of things around me that used to be automatic."

But it's really hard trying to tell the doctors what's actually happening to me because I'm not sure what normal is anymore. Am I mentally or physically sick? In this sport you need all your wits, senses and natural instincts about you. Motorcycle racing, at any level, demands complete and total concentration. Anything less and you're a danger not only to yourself, but also to those competing for track space with you. I think my competitors take it for granted how developed these fine senses are. I suppose this is what most people would call natural ability. So I found it hard to talk to my rivals about my condition. They are the competition, and it's their job to beat me, beat "mighty Honda". So I'm hardly going to alert them I'm no longer up to it at the moment. Especially now I'm 34 and reaching an age where people usually quit racing at the highest level. I know that the permanent hangover I'm living with has nothing to do with my age or fitness, and so far the tests have proved it. Anyone who knows me knows that I'll work on things until I work it out. I'll lie awake at night analysing just how I can improve either my riding performance or the bike. That's the way I am. Yet this is something that's never happened to me before. There's something definitely wrong, and not knowing what it is scares the shit out of me. Just because you're turning 34, you don't suddenly grow old overnight, but that's the way I feel. Waking up this morning, it was like I'd aged 20 years overnight.

The doctors had tried me on a super carbohydrate diet to give me instant energy to help with my preseason training. It was equal to eating 26 slices of bread a day and I knew this was getting me nowhere. All through my career I'd tried different diets. I've always been a believer in everything in moderation while focusing on my racing. So I tried the high carb diet again, but it didn't help my condition.

I had even called two-time World 500cc Champion Barry Sheene, who now lives in Australia. My wife Megan and I had read an article that said he suffers from CFS. Barry's symptoms were similar to mine and he said the only thing that really helped him was to have a 20-minute cold bath every morning. So in the week of the last round of the 1999 Superbike championship at Sugo in Japan, I got up every morning and had a 20-minute cold bath. But the bath did bugger all except make me feel cold for the rest of the day. I lost second place in the 1999 championship on race day.

My wife Megan was the only one living my personal hell with me, and who understood what I had been going through for months. I called her in New Zealand and told her I had parked the bike. She knew instantly I had now reached desperation point. We have been together nearly all my racing career, and she knows me better than anyone else. When she heard I'd walked out of the test session she knew right away the problem was now more serious than ever before. It obviously wasn't the pressure and stress of testing for she knew I'd always been willing to grit my teeth and get on with the job before. Each scar on my body is testimony to a racer's will to win. I've stretched leather gloves and boots over swollen, bleeding, and broken hands and feet in the past, and simply got on with the painful job of racing. It's what professional motorcycle racers do for a living.

I asked her to get all the medical notes from my doctors in New Zealand and fax them to Australia. She was preparing to leave Wellington and I was supposed to connect with her in Sydney, then fly on to Europe to start the 2000 World Superbike season. Yet thoughts of the racing ahead are the last thing on my mind.

It's requiring all my concentration just to keep this damn rental car in a straight line, and stop hitting the cats' eyes. I knew the minute I woke this morning this was no normal Valentine's Day for Megan and me. I'd gone to bed early with my traditional comfort meal of tomato soup via room service, as I had been doing for the last few weeks at about 9 pm and then was sleeping till 9 am the next day. So I was really getting lots of sleep, but waking up feeling really shit. This morning I woke up with a bad headache and I couldn't actually see. I couldn't focus, the room was dark. There was morning light filtering through the curtains, but I couldn't seem to see anything. This wasn't the Aaron Slight who had been placed ahead of rugby star Jonah Lomu as the most successful sportsman on a New Zealand business paper's Rich List. This wasn't the Aaron Slight who had almost won the World Superbike Championship six times. Nor was it the person who'd won, three times in a row, the gruelling Suzuka 8-Hour endurance race, motorcycle racing's equivalent of the Tour de France. No, it was me at my lowest, most vulnerable moment.

Motorcycle racers are sports people in pain denial. There's no health plan in this year-to-year profession. The stakes are high in motorcycle racing at the top level. The British-based team I ride for has an annual budget of millions of pounds, and the two contracted riders are the pivots of that investment. If we can't ride to the best of our ability, then it's just a matter of time before the bikes get handed to someone more capable of winning. Win at all costs is motorcycle racing's motto, and it suffers the sick poorly.

It took quite a few minutes for the room to lighten even though my eyes were open. I still had double vision, which felt weird and disorientating.

It was as if I had been on the booze for a week and couldn't balance. It was so bad, I had trouble dressing, and yet there I was, getting up to go and ride one of the fastest, most expensive motorbikes in the world for hours at the Eastern Creek circuit, Sydney. So I'm telling myself the old motto - "when the going gets tough, the tough get going".

When I arrive at the track everybody's mingling around. It's the first day of the three-day test, and my teammate Colin Edwards and I are going to put the new V-twin through its paces, just as we had done the week before at Phillip Island near Melbourne. In fact, Phillip Island had been OK. I wasn't feeling great but the times were good. I've always recorded my times in my diary and they weren't bad. It was a mixed field of World Superbike and Japanese domestic championship riders, and I was 0.747 of a second behind Itoh on the Honda Twin on the first cool morning of the test session. By the last day I was second fastest in the afternoon, the higher air temperatures closer to race conditions.

However, when arriving this morning at Eastern Creek I felt my world was closing in. As I put on my leathers I felt I hadn't really woken up. The whole team are there. They have all come out from England especially for this test and Honda's future in World Superbikes is riding on how Colin and I perform. Normally that's no pressure, and I'd been waiting my whole Superbike career of almost 13 years to ride a twin. I'd always felt that the larger engine size ceiling given to twins by World Superbike rules created opportunities for more torque and traction. I'd finally got the chance to ride Honda's interpretation of a 1000cc four-stroke twin-cylinder racebike, but as I exited the pits for the first time that morning, I wasn't the usual pull-the-pin Aaron.

I did six or eight laps, but it wasn't my usual four quick ones, then back into the pit to change a setting to try to go faster. Usually I go out, settle in, let rip with one flier, then a second, and by the third or fourth lap I'm within a second of my best time. I suppose I should have pulled in there and then, but I 'm a stubborn bastard, and I just didn't want to admit defeat. I was hoping that, like the times I rode injured, I could just put the problem to the back of my mind and get on with what Honda was paying me for. People close to me were saying it was all in my head and I just had to get over it.

Turning into turn four there are some really bad bumps and the vibration of the front wheel shakes up my vision really bad. It's like my brain can't keep up with the vibration. It's on overload. It can't stabilise the vibration of the bike so all I'm seeing is a buzzy blur as I'm going into the turn. I'm tipping it in through feel and instinct, not by what I can see. I've been through there a million times before and I know the corner goes that way, and where the bumps are. I'm going by feel. I do the laps but I'm about 6 seconds off the pace. I'm never 6 seconds off the pace. Six seconds in bike terms, when you race for a living, is like a wet week in my Wairarapa home territory. An eternity. In my whole Honda career I've never been 6 seconds off the pace. And I'm thinking well, maybe I just need a good fix of caffeine or something. It was like I was riding around with a tear off on my visor that has water smeared between them. It was speed at its most surreal.

It really began to scare me, and as I tried to go faster I finally gave in to what ever it was that was making me feel this way. I'm not a person who likes to admit defeat. My hands tell anyone that. The left wrist has around

60 percent movement, the right hand two tendons for four fingers and a pinkie that'd scare Captain Hook. Then there was the night I fell asleep in a chair with these two swollen meathooks in buckets of ice before a Suzuka 8-Hour. I'd smacked them so hard into the track in a practice crash that the team was amazed I showed up to race. First I had to get up early to pay a visit to Kushitani to get them to expand my gloves with extra leather panels, so they would fit over the swelling. Even with uninjured hands, Suzuka is long and hard enough to blacken the nails of your braking fingers. We won.

As I said, I don't like giving up. It's the same for all riders at this level. It's just not in our make-up to wave the white flag. Focus and sheer bloody-minded determination is what makes all of us tick. I've spent the last 14 years since I left New Zealand focussing my every hour on getting to, then winning, the World Championship. Now I'm six seconds off the pace on the new bike, and the bike is fine. The problem is me.

I come into the pits after just 10 minutes of the session, and as I get off the bike I'm choking back tears. By now I have hit desperation point and I say to the guys in the team: "I just don't know what's going on, I just have no idea but if I ride the bike anymore today I'm going to hurt myself."

As always my team is very supportive and they can't figure it out either. They gather around me as they do at the end of every session. My new chief mechanic Chris Pike, engine builder Mark Lloyd, chassis man Simon Greer and Simon Stubbs are all looking at me for answers and I am looking back at their expectant faces. Plus there's the team manager Neil Tuxworth and, as it's a Honda test, all the important people from

Honda in Japan are there too. Our press officer Chris Herring is there and he must be wondering how he can put a positive spin on this.

First I talk to my chief mechanic Chris and the mechanics of the team, trying to explain the situation. Trying to explain how bad I feel. I don't know what's going on, and they can't help me. I'm asking for help, probably for the first time in my life, and I am saying, what can I do? Of course, these people know me better than most. We spend our lives together. They surround me every time I get off the bike, gathering information and answers, that's how it works in bike racing. Normally I'm an animated fountain of feedback. Today I'm struck dumb.

I usually ride bikes to the absolute limit of their capabilities until the machine can't take it anymore. Testing is all about finding a way to set the bike up so you can race it flat out on the very limit for a 100km race without it breaking or something falling off. It's simple really. It's all about getting to that point, that balance between peak performance, bike failure, and the potential to crash. It's a very fine line and it takes hours of testing. Yet my team at Honda is one of the best in the world, and when we're not going in the right direction, we gather around and analyse the data and the settings to try to work out what we have to change. When I'm off the pace of the fastest time we look at the data and they listen to my feedback and decide what the solution should be. Electronic telemetry can only tell the mechanics so much; human feedback is vital. The bike is then pulled apart and modified to the new settings. It's the process the team and I have been going through for years. That's why we're all scratching our heads looking at each other because I am unable to play my part. I suppose I had been treating my situation like a bike test. Seeing all those doctors for the last eight months, analysing all the data and hoping that the answer would be found so we could all get on with our jobs. Up until that point I had struggled through on the bike, had still come up with good results and still gone fast. Now I was six seconds off the pace and had no answers. Neither did the team.

By now, though, I feel I'm going insane. I have been questioning my own mental stability through all this. Concussion is a regular event for a go-hard motorcycle racer. Was that a factor?

I've been motorcycle racing for a long time and maybe the stress of working so hard for so long is getting to me and I'm going loopy. I'm second-guessing myself, and everybody around me is trying to be helpful. They're saying, it's nothing, it's nothing, you'll be right, which is really the last thing I wanted to hear. I'm glad that I was listening to myself and my own inner belief because if I'd listened to them, with the way I was feeling, I would have thrown myself off a bridge. I wanted it to be something serious. It felt serious, and when everybody says you're fine it becomes confusing. By now I was feeling so low I even had thoughts of topping myself.

So I go and explain to my team manager Neil Tuxworth that I can't carry on with the testing. It wasn't an easy thing to do because I knew just how important the new V-twin was to the team.

He questions me, but I can't honestly tell him what's wrong. We probably spent half an hour deliberating about what I should do. He suggests that maybe I should contact his doctor who fixed him up in his race days. Dr Witek Mintowt-Czyz had also helped me with my finger injury from the collision with Colin at Donington in '99.

I've always been one to worry about what people think of me, and I try to get along with everybody. So now I'm thinking that, if the team thought John Kocinski was weird with his hygiene obsession, what must they be thinking of me. I'm sure they thought I'd lost it.

So I left the track and headed for the doctors again. What else could I do? Luckily, one of my best friends, Rob Phillis, lives in Sydney. We had been teammates in my Kawasaki days, when I was riding in Australia and the world championship. We'd been friends ever since.

I drove the rental car to his place. I asked Rob's wife Carol if it was OK to stay at their house that night. I explained I wasn't feeling at all on to it. Rob came home from work and drove me to my hotel where I grabbed my bags and checked out. By this stage I couldn't drive myself. All that evening I was feeling worse and worse. They didn't know what was going on either and were very supportive. Like everyone else they were saying you'll be all right. I remember turning to Rob and Carol and saying: "Well, actually I hope they do find something wrong with me because if they don't, I'm in deep shit. I can't go on like this."

It was more comforting being with them than being stuck in a hotel room by myself. Megan was on her way over the next morning and the medical notes had been sent through. At this stage I was still considering meeting the connection and continuing with her to Europe, as there'd still been nothing definite about what was wrong with me. I might still be OK. Maybe I could see a doctor in Europe.

The next day I go to see Doctor Sharon Flahive. She's got all my medical notes from New Zealand and, after seeing all these doctors over the last eight months, they're starting to form a small book. In hindsight, it's quite ironic that on the last page of this mountain of notes was a handwritten note from the doctor in New Zealand, Dr Ruth Highet, saying: " Thanks for squeezing him in. He's a lovely guy, and a non-complainer! He has had no head-imaging yet."

By head imaging, Dr Highet meant a brain scan. I'd had a CT scan, but only for my body. So we talked and we agreed I better get a brain scan. Dr Flahive got me an appointment for 8.45am the next morning. A brain scan is not a pleasant thing. They put you in this MRI machine and run you back and forth and it's really noisy. But, strangely, I was not the least bit anxious. The scanner operators warned me that it would be weird and claustrophobic, "so try not freak out too much".

It turned out to be one of my most relaxing times in months. I instinctively knew that at last the doctors were on the right track, getting to the top, rather than the bottom, of what was wrong with me. My grandad's death from bowel cancer had initially started the search for the cause of my condition at the other end of my body.

I had a real sense of calm. I thought: "To hell with everybody else. I know there's something wrong inside my head. And this machine will finally tell me what it is."

It was supposed to take 10 to 15 minutes. But I'm looking at the clock on the wall and I've been in the MRI for more than half an hour. There must be something wrong because I should have been out ages ago. Yet I still feel strangely comforted because I know they have found something. It is in my head, after all. Just like everyone has been saying. I'm not a nut case.

I'm looking forward to getting out so I can tell everyone. My team, my friends, and especially Megan, that I really hadn't lost the plot. Sometimes you just need a decent excuse and this was the excuse of all excuses. A get-out-of-the-mental-hospital-free card.

But when I get out of the MRI, no one will tell me anything. They say come back tomorrow to get the test results. I try to tell them I haven't got the time to come in tomorrow as I'm catching a flight to Europe. They say no, we can't read the tests. The guy who actually took the photos and did the MRI scan has passed the information on to the doctor. I find him in a room, reading the results, and typing them up. I wait until he finishes the work, then plead to be told what is wrong with me. He says: "Well, it's best to go back to your doctor and she can explain what we've found but I can tell you we have discovered a bleed and it's about 2 centimetres in size. You need to go back to your doctor to discuss how to deal with this."

A bleed of any sort on the brain is known as a stroke. I've basically had a stroke and I didn't know it. All this time I've been testing the bike at Phillip Island and now here in Sydney, part of my brain has been saturated with blood. I start trying to work out when the blood vessel burst, and I realise it was probably a week ago in the surf at Phillip Island. I went out boogie boarding with some of the mechanics on a day off from testing. Normally I would have stayed in for longer, but after three waves I developed a huge headache, and had to get out of the water. I was looking back across the water into the sun's rays, which were piercing my pupils. It felt like the reflection was killing my eyes. The piercing feeling was going straight back into my brain and I thought I can't be in this water any longer. I get out and sit and wait for the guys to finish. That was probably it. That was probably the explosion of blood inside my head. Through most of the previous race season, I had been feeling increasingly dull due to the pressure building up in one part of my brain. After the mechanised violence of motorcycle racing, it took a peaceful day's surfing to trigger my own internal volcano.

The next day had been another day off riding because we were doing some PR photos. Then, on the following weekend, there was the V8 Supercars at Phillip Island so I'd stayed to watch friend and fellow Kiwi Greg Murphy drive in the premier class of four-wheeled racing down under. On the Sunday I had flown up to Sydney to start the Eastern Creek phase of the test programme. I wasn't feeling good the whole time, even when I was watching the V8s. I'd go out for the qualifying and come back to the hotel between sessions so that I could get out of the sun and rest my head and have a wee nap.

So as I'm sitting there in the doctor's office in Sydney, it's all starting to make sense. The medical jigsaw was starting to form a picture. The doctor says all I can do now is get onto a specialist in this area. I'm starting to visualise scenarios where they drill a hole in your skull and drain the blood off. It must be a simple process to get rid of it, and that's that. The doctor refers me to Professor Michael Morgan, who is actually in California at the time, lecturing on his favourite subject - the brain. But he is due back in Sydney the next day, so I'm booked to see him as soon as he arrives. It is now Wednesday night, and I'm looking forward to seeing Megan.

Back at the Phillis house. Robbie has gone to the airport to pick up Megan who I'd talked to as soon as I'd learnt about the 2cm bleed. I told her to check her bags only as far as Sydney, as I may have to have an operation - still being unsure how my brain will be fixed. Carol has to go and pick up daughter Georgia. So in typical Phillis style, I'm left looking after the other kids, Tommy and Alex, for half an hour while Carol collects her. This is the way it has always been because Megan and I are extensions of the Phillis family, and it's just like babysitting our own nieces, nephews, sons or daughters. They have all become special people in our lives. But while Carol's out I get a call from the doctor, who says: "I don't think you should be at home tonight. You should go and admit yourself to hospital." I ask what is this all about because I'm still guessing it's a simple, routine thing. She says, it could get worse, or get better, but she wants me checked in tonight for safety's sake.

Megan arrives and we get in the car and go to the hospital. Typically, hospitals take about two hours to find you a bed. No change here. I stay overnight on Wednesday because I won't be able to see the doctor until Thursday night when he gets back from California.

As Thursday morning rolls round the first person I see is Megan and the conversation quickly centres on getting me out of this hospital. I have just spent the night with three other patients on a noisy ward in a public hospital. As the seriousness of the situation sets in I want my own space. So Megan sets about getting me into a private hospital where Professor Morgan also operates. The only thing to do that day was to have an angiograph then see the professor. This is the first time I feel my life is in danger, and the comfort of yesterday's knowledge is being replaced by a growing fear for the future. Before I go into theatre for the angiograph I must sign my life away due to the risks involved during this procedure. The doctor says there's a small percentage of death, further strokes or possible paralysis. An angiograph is where they stick a huge needle in your groin finding a main artery. They then force it all the way up to the base of your skull, and release the dye to check for other possible malfunctioning veins in the brain. The bonus of this procedure is the free bikini wax. The negative is the possibility of an early send- off in the game called Life. The big D.

When Professor Morgan arrives we talk about what we're going to do. He says there are three options. You can leave it. You can use radiation to get rid of it, but the bleed should be within 1cm so that's not really an option as mine is twice the size. The final option is to operate. So, not really knowing what the operation is, I'm still thinking that all they're going to do is drill into the side of my head and drain the blood seepage, like removing the contaminated oil from a bike engine. But there's no real choice for me - just get it out of my head, professor; let's get on with it. I feel positive I've finally found out what the problem is, and all we've got to do is to have a simple operation and everything should be sweet.

But there's no such thing as simple brain surgery, and I still hadn't grasped how serious things were. My life was now more under threat than at any time racing motorcycles. I was so focused on finally getting an answer on what was wrong and relieved that I wasn't going mad, that I hadn't fully appreciated the facts. Strangely I felt better than I had for a while because of this sense of calm. I just wasn't fighting it any more, because I was finally getting some answers.

I didn't realise how stressed I'd become with worry. I'd be out training on pushbike rides thinking it's too hard - it shouldn't be this hard, looking for a bit of support. I kept telling myself you've been through it before, you've done it before, you've just got to toughen up and get on with it. And so you do, you toughen up, put the pain and the setbacks aside and get on with reaching for life's glittering prizes. Then eventually the pressure just cracks you and wears you down and you wake up one day thinking maybe I am just getting old. Is this what's happening? Is that why there are no older racers because they've reached 34 and then they're old? Does it happen overnight or is it because I'm not focussed enough on what I'm doing - do I need to be more focussed? Do I need to eat more carbohydrates? Do I have bowel cancer? Is my heart all right? All these things were going through my head while going on punishing pushbike rides training for the 2000 season, training that used to be easy. I ride long and hard because that's what I do to keep fit. It had started as fun, but now it was hard work. So when I finally knew I had this bleed I didn't feel scared, I felt relieved.

The final diagnosis confirmed that I'd been true to my intuition and myself. That was a real lesson in life for me. Well two lessons actually. Lesson one - always get a second opinion. Don't trust any diagnosis that doesn't match what you're feeling. Nobody likes going to doctors, especially me, and particularly when it looks like I'm being a hypochondriac and they're all telling me how fit and healthy I am. The frustration of seeing doctors all over the world, from Italy to England, Australia and New Zealand, and getting nowhere, had finally paid off after eight months of anguish. Lesson two - don't give up on your inner feelings. They may one day save your life.

Professor Morgan was so calm and matter of fact about my options that he really put me at ease. My attitude straight away was right, let's have the operation and let's get this problem sorted. I wasn't thinking about bikes at all. I should have flown to Monaco the day before to continue my preparation for the new season ahead, which was starting in a month's time. Let's get this dealt to, I thought, so I can get back to my life and my racing. Like most people I work hard at what I do and I just wanted to get back to being able to do it to my full potential. I had no thoughts about how dangerous the operation would be, hanging up my helmet for good, or anything like that. I race motorcycles fast for a living and over the years I've been damn good at it. What else would I do? Racing has come naturally as I have spent my whole life hooning around on bikes and in cars.

two

Just a Hoon · The Early Days

My journey as a motorcycle racer took me from Masterton near the southern tip of New Zealand's North Island to the principality of Monaco. I now reside in the latter, but Masterton is where the adventure started. It's a small town of 19,500 people serving a surrounding sheep-farming and winemaking community, and while it's easy to take the man out of Masterton, it's harder to take Masterton out of the man.

Small town New Zealand shaped and formed me. Even when strolling amongst the super yachts moored in Monaco on a sunny August day, I'm wondering about the effects of winter on the Wairarapa valley, and its main town. Masterton is about seven hours drive from Auckland or, in my 400 bhp Holden V8 Ute, around four and a half. The nearest city is the capital, Wellington, an hour and a quarter away, across the Rimutaka Hills.

Growing up in Masterton I lived in two family homes, the second built by my parents on the east side of town. This house was my parents' pride and joy. So much so we all had jobs to do to keep it ship-shape and my Dad was always working on improvements. My Mum was very house-proud and Phillipa, my elder sister, and I both had set tasks to do. My pet hate was vacuuming my room, which had shag pile carpet. I had to vacuum it with the head off and, once finished, rake it. I have taken this habit through life with me and you can still find me, head off the vacuum, going through our motorhome or apartment with a fine toothcomb. Another job was weeding the lawn by hand. It might seem a waste of time in these days of weed-sprays, but picking out the weeds with my young fingers was a sort of quest for perfection, one I carried through to my racing. Where other teammates would accept a mediocre bike set-up, I'd keep on trying to get it right.

My mother Jill was a part time secretary working for the YMCA. She is a very interesting and caring woman. However, I do have her to thank for some of my obsessive-compulsive traits. She would never admit to it these days, as she is so different now. It took the break-up of my parents' marriage for her to really spread her wings. My mother wasn't there a lot for my teenage years, and we have a unique relationship, not your typical mother/son one. I have never resented her leaving the family to find herself, and the one thing I always feel from my Mum, and that she always makes clear, is her love.

My father Rex worked at the local sawmill in charge of the yard. He was a hard worker and not a pub stop out. He was always home shortly after work to participate in the end of the family day. Sometimes it would be to discipline the kids. Whenever we crossed the line, my mother would say, "Wait until your father gets home!" As an adult, I value the lessons I learnt through their discipline.

I think I take after my Dad. We both see things in black and white, right or wrong, there's no grey area in the middle. My father taught me humility, which kept me grounded through all the success in my career. His first thoughts are for others and their needs. He has a quiet way of being helpful and caring without losing his strength of presence. I have seen people's success cloud their character, this could never happen to my Dad, and he would never let it happen to me. I am proud to be my father's son.

Phillipa is two years older than me and is now married to Ejvind and they have two children, Maddisen and Bjarne. Phillipa and I have always been close, the best of friends. I really cannot explain the bond between us, but the tie was probably strengthened when Mum left. We all just got on with life domestically, filling in the hole Mum left behind in our lives. Phillipa has always seemed to know more about me than sometimes I think I know myself. Megan, Ejvind, Maddisen and Bjarne now share the same special bond.

My sister and I watched each other's backs and there was definitely no tale telling on each other as the consequences could be painful. My Dad used to believe in the 'spare the rod, spoil the child' theory. As a result we learned young to stick together. I still haven't told Dad that Phillipa broke the toilet door while on hands and knees throwing up in the bowl - oops, sorry Sis, just had to break the habit of a lifetime there...

To make a living out of racing motorbikes would be a fairytale dream for someone growing up in Masterton during the '80s. The only real goal I ever set myself was to give whatever I participated in my all. Maybe it's a trait I learnt from my parents who were keen sportspeople.

They played basketball and occasionally attended local tournaments. I played basketball and rugby, and did gymnastics at the YMCA, along with trampoline aerobatics. Everyday, it seemed, I would be doing some sort of sport, which was quite usual growing up in a small New Zealand town.

Mum had a love of horses, and tried to get me into it, but it wasn't really me. Phillipa, however, was keen and had a horse of her own. Mum managed to find a horse needing to be kept in shape, so that was my job. It was my first real introduction to horsepower. The two-wheeled horses I ride these days are probably more controllable even though, in power terms, there are around 185 of them under me at once. Even so, I learned to ride quite well, although it was still a chore to me. It was mutual; the horses weren't so rapt about me either.

One day when Phillipa and her friend Adele galloped off down the river track, I set out to prove that Piedy, my trusty steed, was every bit as fast as their nags. The fact that Piedy was only half as tall was even more reason to "smoke 'em". Once she started galloping, I couldn't stop her. Piedy had a mind of her own and didn't stop until she was well out in front. So far in front she had bolted straight over the main road, and finally pulled up in the middle of the Horseshoe Pub roundabout that day. I left hoof prints on the grass in the middle of the roundabout, and it would only be a couple of years before they turned into wheel tracks. I had just experienced my first taste of speed.

Small town New Zealand in those days was all about the outdoors and being active. Masterton seemed to largely consist of average and lower income earners who were just trying to get by and have a bit of fun on their hard-earned weekends. It was a simple life and the surroundings were your main source of entertainment. When I was a kid there were no such things as PlayStations or videos. Even television was a rare treat. In our house, TV was never allowed after school. I remember we always had the choice to either go to bed before the six o'clock news or after watching it - what a choice! Can you imagine a 10-year-old today going to bed at seven o'clock?

At weekends I always got up earlier than anyone else. The central heating grate would have the laundry hanging above it but I would climb under the washing and zoom around the grate with my matchbox toys. I always looked after the toys as I knew, if they were damaged or lost, it would be hard to get another. Friends definitely never took them outside. I had no real aspirations of racing cars or bikes back then, but had the cars sliding through the obstacles as they did on the *Starsky and Hutch* TV show, revelling in the lack of traction of plastic wheels on metal.

At primary school I hung out with the sportier kids and we would kick the rugby ball over the posts, play marbles or just muck around. The best sport of all was 'feelies' - running up behind some poor girl and groping her budding breasts. (That game lasted only a few weeks before the headmaster disciplined us.) When I took part in school sports I was always very competitive. Maybe I wasn't the strongest, biggest or fastest kid in the game, but I always pushed to my limit and beyond to succeed. I was a very confident sportsperson and sport was my way of showing off.

I was very small for my age and didn't really grow until I was about 15. You could always tell the small guys in the class; in school photos we were always put on the end of the girls' line. Boy, I hated that!

Like most New Zealand kids I enjoyed rugby and I always played on the wing. I often tell Megan that if I hadn't raced bikes I could have been an All Black. Why not? You need some goals. Many years later I competed against All Black first five-eight Andrew Merhtens in a multi-sport obstacle course challenge for New Zealand TV. I smoked him! While I completed a post-race interview standing up, Merhts was on the ground, throwing up from the effort. Halfback was where I really wanted to play, but our coach always put his son in that position. Out on the wing I did score a few tries before chucking it in. I got sick of playing with kids a year younger than me because of my size.

I don't know why but for as long as I have been participating in sport, I've always felt the underdog. Whether it has been the size of my body or the size of my bike engine, it has ultimately forced me to dig deep and give it 100 percent. I don't believe you can give it 110 percent - there's no such thing. Because of my determination I have always pushed hard and sometimes I lost the battle, but I always stuck around for the war. Like most motorcycle racers I have had plenty of injuries - some worse than others. You just get up, survey the damage, kick the bike or the body straight again, and get back on. It has been that way for me since I was a kid. A small town New Zealand childhood is a school of hard knocks.

The injury list starts way before I discovered motorcycles. My first x-rays came when I was a baby and rolled off the kitchen table. That was the first injury, but now I could probably fill the rest of this book describing those that followed, but I'll spare you most of the gory details. I'm glad I learned what pain was early on, and developed a high tolerance of it.

The first sporting injury I can remember happened while I was playing softball with Phillipa. I stabbed the tomato stake we were using as a bat through my left calf. It gave me my first scar. I was screaming for Mum, while walking back to the house with one hand on the stake still stuck in my leg.

My school reports always had good marks for physical education and maths. I enjoyed maths, art, and tech drawing because they were useful and you always had something to show for it. I don't think I'm the only professional racer out there who wasn't academic. Maths, though, proved very helpful to me in my career. It helps to decipher the data and computer readouts of bike telemetry. Data recorders on the bike give us reams of information to sift through and interpret as we strive to improve the set-up of the bike. Yet when it came to books I don't think I ever read one at school. I used to bluff my way through book reviews by reading the back covers and asking a few friends what they were about. I couldn't see the point in reading when you could be outside playing sport.

After school I'd throw my bags off at home, then go ride my pushbike, a Raleigh 20. I would pull wheelies, counting the distance I unicycled by lamp post. I think the record was about six, which would be around 150 metres. I still like to pull wheelies sometimes on my motocross bike, but the best ones are the length of a back straight, with 50,000 Superbike fans watching, as a celebration of a race win.

I've always enjoyed speed, whether it was on my bicycle or on my home built push kart. It was even more fun in the kart if I hosed down the drive leading into the basement garage. Instead of putting my feet down to stop I just spun out on the slippery surface. But there's no obvious source of this passion. My Dad wasn't a speed freak and none of my family had that much interest in motor sport.

On one of our traditional family summer holidays, we all went to the Wanganui circuit to watch the first road race I'd seen. The speed seed may have been sown then. It's a great street racing circuit that runs over railway lines and weaves in and out of the tombstones. At that time, the Wanganui Boxing Day races were part of the Marlboro Series, well-promoted races with enough prize money to attract big international names in the European off-season. Randy Mamola, Pat Hennan, Marco Lucchinelli, Chas Mortimer, Greg Hansford, and other top riders would come over and race. But my favourite that day was Graeme Crosby riding a modified 1000cc Kawasaki which was possibly the world's first Superbike. Other riders like Stu Avant and Randy would ride TZ Yamahas and RGV 500 Suzukis. They were proper racing bikes. It looked weird because all the race bikes would come by with the riders tucked behind the faring in the racing position, hotly pursued by Graeme on the more upright Z1000 with its high handlebars. He would come off of the corners on the back wheel, which was awesome. It was New Zealand's own mini Isle of Man TT.

From that day I was determined to ride a motorcycle. I spent the rest of those holidays pestering my parents whenever I saw a sign advertising minibikes for hire. Dad said, "If you're that keen, why don't you ask Dave?"

It took me about three weeks to pluck up the courage to ask Dave, who was then my aunt's boyfriend (and later my uncle), if I could borrow his

Yamaha GT80MX, which he was either given or swapped for a few dozen beers. Dave didn't object when I finally asked him for a ride. He was a bike fanatic. He had a Kawasaki Z900, probably one of the biggest bikes made at the time. When Dad and I picked up the bike, I was probably more excited than I'd ever been. The bubble burst a little when Dad told me I was never to ride the Yamaha alone. He would teach me to ride it properly.

On the first rides in the grass paddocks adjoining our house, I was only allowed to ride it in first gear. Dad was handing out gears like lollies to a good kid, and soon I was allowed to go into second and then third gear. One day I wanted to go for a ride, but Mum was getting a bit sick of watching me, so she said she would keep an eye on me from the window. I knew she wasn't watching me, so I went really fast and using all the gears until I ended up sticking it into the fence. It hurt, but I couldn't go back home crying or Mum would have taken the bike away. We pulled the bike out of the web of fence wire it was trapped in, and no harm was done.

I was soon bored with riding around the paddock so I talked my father into taking me somewhere different. We went down to the river track, where we met some people who were unloading a bike to check it was okay for the motocross the next day. They were the Blackwood family, and their son Peter would become a great friend of mine.

My father got talking to Mr Blackwood who said, "Why don't you come down to the Gladstone track and have a proper go at junior motocross?" I was chomping at the bit to get there. I even polished up my rubber gumboots the night before. It was the first time I couldn't sleep I was so excited and nervous. It was more fun for the family as we became regulars at motocross events. We would all go, take a picnic and have a good day out. They got hooked as much as I did. We also convinced our family friends - the Henderson's - to come to local meetings and their son Gary would start alongside me. I had none of the proper gear. I used my Dad's helmet, which he wore during the week to go to and from work on his 50cc motorbike. It was open faced and about 10 sizes too big, but we couldn't afford a new one. I was in my jeans, wearing neither gloves nor goggles. You wouldn't get away with it today, but New Zealand was a more casual place back then. We couldn't afford to buy new gear and didn't really see the need for it. My mother didn't clean my boots and gear for me. I learnt from an early age that I had to do all that myself.

My parents were still playing basketball and went on an overseas holiday with the team. It was 1978 and they went to Fiji. Before going they promised to buy me a bike of my own when they returned. For those two weeks Phillipa and I stayed at Nana and Grandad Slight's. Every day I read the motocross magazines and eyed up my new bike. Their trip seemed to take a month, but they were true to their promise. Soon I was the proud owner of a used Yamaha YZ80E.

Soon afterwards I started at Makora College, which I attended for four years, leaving at age 17 with my School Certificate - just. Luckily I got high marks for art and technical drawing. I didn't have any of my long-term friends at my new school so in the third and fourth form I worked hard. By the fifth form I had a couple of really good mates, Waka and Justin. Waka and I used to ride our motorbikes to school every day. This made it very tempting to take the odd class off, and rip down to the river for some serious trail riding. The more classes you skip, the easier it is to take more off, so I spent less and less time at school.

I had started motocross at 12, riding 80s all through my junior days because of my size. At 16, one year after you can get your road licence in New Zealand, you must step up to the senior ranks in motocross. So I had to buy a 125, although I struggled with the bike, which was too tall for me. At the start line I would stand on one tippy toe, with the seat under the opposite thigh to reach the ground. It was hard to get a good start. It was still early days and I wasn't thinking of becoming a professional racer. In those days, growing up in New Zealand, I don't think most people aimed to do anything very specific. In Masterton you just left school, and got a job, whatever you could get.

At 13 I started working at Gregory Motorcycles, the Masterton Yamaha shop, during the school holidays. Once the holidays were finished I started working two hours a day at the bike shop, from 3.30pm to 5.30pm. I now had a regular income and learnt then to spend it very wisely. At 15 I would make $30 a week. $5 for gas, $5 - $7 for beer and entertainment, and the rest banked, as I needed around $13 a week to meet my bike payments. So I was already starting to budget and budget well.

Sometimes the $5 for petrol just wasn't enough. So on a Friday night I'd take a litre out of a couple of farm bikes to top up the tank of my trusty DT175. I did not see it as stealing. I saw it as fair payment for slogging over their dirty bikes. You would think a farmer would hose down his bike before he brought it in to us.

Things changed quickly for me at about 15 years of age. My parents had separated when I was 13, which was a difficult time for us all. This left Dad, Phillipa and I together in the family home. My Dad wanted to settle the marital estate by selling the house. I'm still not sure what impact their separation had on me, but I suppose, at the least, it made me a little apprehensive about marriage. Megan and I were married five years ago after 'living in sin' for 10.

My father saw things very much in black and white. As the relationship was over, it was time to settle up and get on with it. So the house was sold, and Phillipa and I went to live with her boyfriend Ejvind, as we had nowhere else to go. Dad had moved in with a lady friend and was looking for a new home for us all.

I could easily have gone off the rails back then, and I probably would have if it hadn't been for motorcycles. I was now 15, old enough to have a road licence for a car and a motorbike. I had a Yamaha DT175 trail bike to go to school and back on. I was living with Phillipa and Ejvind - who was five years older than me. I made my own rules, and I didn't have to come home if I didn't want to. I also had the use of Dad's old work vehicle - a Morris 1100. Ejvind had become a friend immediately when he helped Phillipa clean up vomit from my bed and the wall of the house outside my window. This was prior to me moving in with them and that night had started with Phillipa and Ejvind going out on a date. Dad was away. I invited Peter around for the night. Peter had his licence so I talked him into letting me ride his Suzuki 90 to the shop to buy a king size cake of peppermint chocolate. I was still 14 and shouldn't have been riding on the road. After returning with the chocolate, it all turned a bit messy when we started mixing up different concoctions of alcohol from my father's stash. We put a nip from each bottle into a Tupperware container, shook it up and drank it all in one gulp. That mixed with the chocolate filled my young stomach with the foulest of pseudo crème de menthe liqueurs. This was my first experience with alcohol - the usual teenage rite of passage. I was hanging out the window throwing up as Phillipa and Ejvind arrived back. Phillipa spotted me, and got Ejvind to hose off the evidence as she saw to me and changed the sheets on my bed. The cover up story we prepared for Dad the next morning was that I'd had another one of my bleeding noses and Phillipa had to put my sheets in the tub to soak. Nowadays, Ejvind and I are more like brothers than in-laws and there is nothing I wouldn't do for him or he for me.

Getting my licence was another rite of passage for me that year. The day I turned 15 I sat the theory for both car and bike and a few days later passed my practicals. As soon as I legally hit the road I was being pulled over. The cops could not believe I had my motorcycle licence because I was so small for my age. It was a hard lesson to learn, but every time I saw police lights I used to flee, which got me in all sorts of trouble. Like the night a policeman knocked on the front door of our family home. I had been on my way home on a Friday night, probably doing about 75km in a 50km zone down Worksop Road. At the Colombo Road intersection I looked back and saw a policeman a long, long way behind. I made a split second decision to make a run for it. I turned up our driveway and am sure to this day he never saw me. I ripped up the driveway, parked the bike in the basement, pulled the roller door down, ran up the stairs, undressed and jumped into bed. As I was jumping in I yelled out to Phillipa, "If anybody knocks on the door I'm not home!"

I was sure the police officer knew me, and where to find me, but he didn't see which way I went. The policeman turned up five minutes later, and knocked on the front door. Phillipa answered. The cop asked to see me but Phillipa, protective as ever, said I was not home. The cop said he had just seen my bike in the garage. Phillipa got me up and I made out I'd been in bed for hours. The cop then proceeded to give me a lecture, but no ticket. I thought afterwards that he had a cheek nosing around in our garage.

I was always being stopped, but in those days you could talk your way out of a ticket. Maybe they saw it as kids having harmless fun. The officer who usually pulled me up was Officer Sanson. He always seemed to be lurking in the wrong place at the wrong time. My DT175 just wasn't grunty enough to blow him off.

My time with Phillipa and Ejvind at the flat lasted about eight months. During this time I had my ear pierced. This lasted about two days, as Dad was still the boss and he soon spotted the earring and insisted I remove it. On Wednesdays, Dad made me join him for dinner where he was staying. After the meal I would borrow his car and take his friend's son, Steven, to the small bore rifle club. On the way we drove past the train station and the car, as though it had a mind of its own, would swerve off into the green grass. We would end up staying there for five or 10 minutes sliding through the wet grass and trees. Steven and I loved Wednesdays. So Dad wouldn't know, we hosed his car down and cleaned it, before going on to the shooting club. That way it had time to dry. I still don't know if he was ever aware of having a cleaner car on Thursday mornings or why. Dad's Nissan 200B also used to go through tyres quite rapidly for some mysterious reason. So I would always manage to talk Dad into getting retreads as I said they were better value for money. With retreads, I had an excuse for them wearing out more quickly. I was skidding the car everywhere, and if a new rear tyre only lasted 10,000 km he would have been suspicious.

The eight months soon went by. Dad had put a successful offer on a more affordable house and it wasn't long before we moved in. Ejvind joined us about 18 months later - he spent all his time with us anyway, so it was pointless him having a flat.

Soon after I turned 17, I was offered a full-time job at Gregory Motorcycles, working alongside Peter. I earned $104 dollars a week, which seemed pretty high at the time. I wanted to make the money to pay off my new Yamaha YZ125J. The shop was owned by Ross and Cushla Gregory, the two people most responsible for kick-starting my motorcycle road racing career. Peter and I were apprentice mechanics and this was my foreseeable future. But I never had the time to sit my final examination, so I'm not a qualified mechanic on paper. This was because every year, when the examinations took place, I was away racing. The exam was always held on the weekend of the Castrol 6-Hour endurance race - an important race in the New Zealand calendar. It was becoming obvious where my priorities lay as I was now seeing bike racing as a possible future.

Peter was a year older than me, so I was probably easily led astray. I was about 18 months behind him in the apprenticeship, and we used to hang out together every weekend, or go to motocross races with our families. Work ended at around 6pm on a Friday. Peter and I would then pool our money along with other friends and go to buy a crate of beer to last us through the weekend. We'd then go back to the bike shop for a couple of drinks with Ross and Cushla. Then we'd race home for a shower and back up town for Friday night 'cruising'. We would do hundreds of laps of Masterton's main street, checking out the talent. My favourite ride used to be up Lansdowne Hill. On the way back down, showing off to friends, we would drag our foot pegs through the turns and watch the sparks fly. What hoons! This was the disapproving term the more mature onlookers used to describe us.

We soon discovered multigrips could be used to clamp off the rear brakes of somebody's car, and do burnouts. Not in my Dad's car, though. Honest. Peter and I, with more friends on bikes, would meet up with mates in cars. This was the time and place where the beer was consumed and the girls fondled. Usually the rendezvous was at the park or the top of Lansdowne Hill. Like most young New Zealand men, I wasn't much good at commitment. Three weeks seeing the same girl was a long time for me. So I knew plenty of girls but they didn't last long. As to the details - they are private and blurry among the wine and the song. Also, girls were expensive and so were my bikes. There had to be a choice. So love 'em and leave 'em became my motto. After all, I was only 17.

Before working as a mechanic I'd had one job interview for a sign-writing job, which I didn't get. Failure isn't something I accept easily. I don't like rejection of any sort so I wasn't about to apply for another 15 jobs with the same result. So I took the first thing that came up - the job with the Gregorys - and ran with it as hard as I could. Looking back, I'm really glad to have a detailed understanding of how the machines I ride work.

Without this mechanical grounding, I wouldn't have been able to work on my own bikes in the early days, which helped me get to where I am today. It also gave me an advantage long after I reached a point where I never had to twirl a spanner again. At the end of each test session as a factory rider, mechanics with different skills swarm around, each wanting to know the answers to their questions, all with the object of getting the bike go quicker. Knowing just a little about what all of them do kept me in good stead throughout my career.

I have the Gregorys to thank for a lot of encouragement. Gregory Motorcycles was my first and only New Zealand sponsor, and I am eternally grateful for their support. Ross also helped in my early motocross days. He lived opposite us and the Motatoa Scout den. Instead of getting annoyed with the kid endlessly buzzing around the scout den's paddocks, Ross showed some interest in me and my GT80, one day showing up to tell me how to clean it properly. It was the first of many lessons he gave to me. In the latter years when I went road racing, we would pack up the shop's van and he would drive all over New Zealand with his whole family in tow - Cushla and daughters Angela and Joanne. He not only provided bikes and spares, he also supported me with his spare time. I hold a lot of fond memories of them all, and I'm very proud of what we achieved together. Together, we certainly kicked some big-city bike shop butt.

My friend Peter Blackwood began road racing first, also with help from Ross. He bought a Yamaha RD250LC and was good immediately. So I decided to have a go at a local club day. All I had was my motocross bike - the YZ125J Yamaha, the first of the water-cooled versions. So I put on some road tyres, geared it right up, and headed to Manfield, the closest road circuit to Masterton.

It was a club day, so there were all sorts of bikes there from 1000s all the way down to my 125. Peter had his RD 250 and the races were open. So we just hooned around. I'd carve up people on the infield in the corners and then they'd blow by me on the straights again. I had a great day. I crashed once, and still have the scar on my knee to prove it. Towards the end of the day the bike had seized. I had wrecked the motor, but still had the biggest of grins on my face. I was now totally hooked on road racing. I returned to Gregory Motorcycles, fixed up my YZ125, and sold it on. At the time I was selling my bike the shop had a YZ250K which had been traded in, and Peter and I took turns sharing it. One week he would ride it, the next I would or we shared it on the same day, racing in different classes. Peter was now becoming a very good road racer and had sold his RD to update it with a RZ350.

He had also traded in his DT175 to buy a XT550. It was an ex-farm bike, a big hulking four-stroke single. We thought it was too heavy to be any good at motocross, so we were planning to take part in the annual flat track race at the Clareville showgrounds. Flat track is not so common in New Zealand, so it was a bit of fun for us. The general rule was to go flat out around a big, flat oval. There was only one rule. You were not allowed to use the brakes, so we took off our front and rear brake levers. Peter decided to ride his XT, which meant I could ride the free YZ250. The 250 two-stroke would be the better bike for the class. It started off as a fun day, and ended in tragedy. Peter lost his life that day.

It was late in the day and we were starting a new race. As we headed for the first corner I was leading the race, but there was a huge pile-up behind as the following bikes tangled handlebars as everyone tried to get a good line. Peter crashed and may have been hit accidentally. It was a huge shock to complete the first lap, and see Peter out cold. I chucked my bike to the ground and ran to him. He was already in a hell of a state, as he didn't seem to be breathing and was turning blue. The doctor and ambulance people arrived very quickly. The doctor jumped into action and it looked like he knew what he was doing. I don't really remember much more than that they rushed him to hospital in the ambulance. My friends and I were not sure of his condition, so we immediately packed up and returned to Masterton hospital to check. It wasn't good. He was in a coma and on a ventilator. It suddenly struck home how serious the injuries were. It all seemed so crazy after some of the stunts we had pulled and gotten away with. This was an organised, seemingly harmless, fun day out for us. From that day on, we waited and prayed for a change in his condition. His parents were constantly at his bedside. I went to see him every morning before work and returned in the evening. About five days later, Peter was struggling to hold his own and then slipped away.

The tragedy of my best friend's death hit us all hard. We all still talk about Peter and remember him in our stories of the early years. I have always felt that my continued racing would have been with his blessing. And I often wonder what he might have achieved if he had lived. He was fast and brave, and could have gone to the very top of the sport.

three

I Landed on My Feet

Unfortunately, a tragic teenage death involving a motor vehicle isn't a rarity in rural New Zealand, where we tend to see engines as an opportunity for entertainment, and an escape from boredom. But Peter's death still hit us hard. There were six to seven guys as close to Peter as I was, and while his funeral gave us some opportunity to express our grief, most of us kept it inside, and tried to get on with our lives. Many Kiwis don't show their emotions enough, and although we didn't hold back the tears at the funeral, it's amazing how we tend to consider grief an expression of weakness. I guess we don't want to appear vulnerable, and don't want to show our sensitivity. At that stage, I hadn't even lost a grandparent. This was my first association with death.

Every time he raced, Peter would come home and tell us how he was doing. We'd be in awe of his tales, like the time he was dicing for the lead on the RZ350 with the big boys at the national title round at the Pukekohe circuit, near Auckland. Peter had just passed Auckland's Rod

Harris and Wellington's Eddie Kattenburg round the outside of the sweeper leading onto the front straight on the grass, but lost the lead shortly after when he put the bike over the fence. He was getting noticed with rides like that, and people were wondering how far this teenager from little old Masterton could go. Peter was on form, and showing his promise at one of the best times on the New Zealand scene.

It was a golden age of racing because a whole lot of things came together at the same time. There was plenty of work around, and plenty of cheap yet cheerful road bikes that could be raced in a number of classes catering for them. It didn't cost the earth to go racing back then. As I remember it a brand new RZ350 cost about $5,000, and you didn't have to do anything to it at all. You'd simply take the speedo off, wire a few things up, maybe put softer compound tyres on if you had the budget, and go for it. That's why every successful racer to emerge from New Zealand honed their skills on production bikes. You couldn't go out and buy a proper TZ Yamaha or RG500 Suzuki race bike because it would cost stupid money. Nor was there any point when you could ride a road bike with 30 other guys racing the same bike, or its closest competitor, and the close racing sharpened up your race craft. When you cleaned up in New Zealand, there was an even more competitive production racing scene beckoning, a short hop across the Tasman in Australia. By contrast, the racing classes were not really strong at all.

About six months after Peter's death, Ross suggested I have a go at road racing. I had cleaned up Peter's battle-scarred RZ350, put the lights and speedo back on, and prepared it for sale as a road bike. I was immediately interested, although the thought of using Peter's bike was a little strange at the time. Despite that reservation, I decided to give it my best shot. So I suggested to Ross, since all the road gear was still on the RZ, that maybe I should ride it to my motorcycle apprenticeship course, and back, a couple of times. I was then doing a two-week Polytech course in Lower Hutt, a smaller dormitory city near Wellington. It used to take about an hour and 10 minutes to drive there in my car so I knew the road well. It was the first time I'd ever ridden a road bike, and the tight and twisty 20-kilometre section over the Rimutaka hill was good practice in chucking the RZ around. There were heaps of hairpins and blind corners to provide plenty of challenge to my riding skill. One day I got up early and dressed in a pair of borrowed leathers, my motocross boots and an Arai Freddie Spencer replica helmet. I took it pretty easy getting to Tech, holding it all back for the Rimutakas on the return trip. All day at Tech, I thought about the ride home and how I could string the corners together better. That road ride on the RZ was the first time I had ridden anything with any decent horsepower and it was awesome fun.

Tech finished for the day at 5 o'clock. It was late winter so it was getting dark around 6-6.30pm. That evening I was winding down the Rimutakas. It was a great ride. Coming into the small town of Featherston, I backed off for the town's 50 km/h speed limit. The sun had left Featherston in the shadow of the hills long ago, and everybody had their lights on, including me. In the middle of the town there is a park with an old steam engine. The main road to Masterton goes straight past it, but there is a fork at the park. Approaching this intersection, an old bloke coming towards me veered his car across the road to take this fork without giving way to me. He didn't indicate so I thought he was going to go straight by me. Wrong. I hit his Morris 1100 square between the headlights, the impact launching me over the top of the car. I did a full somersault, the glancing blow of my head on the Morrie's roof leaving paint on my helmet. Then I landed on my feet. But only for a split second before face planting the road. It wouldn't be the last time a motorcycle seat ejected me into the air, but landing on my feet became a signature of my later race crashes. Perhaps it was due to the gymnastics I did as a kid.

I remember coming around and looking up into the night sky. There were several people's faces hanging over me. I asked one, "Whose fault was it?" His answer, "Not yours" was enough for me to relax back into the gutter and wait for the ambulance. When it arrived, they put us both in, and we set off on the 30-minute journey to Masterton hospital, a lonely siren echoing through a crisp, clear winter night. On the way, the old bloke sounded as though he was dying. It was tempting to tell him to go and rest in peace. The hospital put us in the same ward and the same room. By this time I had no sympathy for the old bastard, as I'd found out he'd been on his way home from the local pub. All night he was moaning and groaning. All I could think about was getting up to give him something to really moan about. The next morning he discharged himself with no injury, the trip to hospital having taken him out of the drink-drive spotlight. Meanwhile I'm stuck in hospital with two broken feet. And I had hit the ground so hard it loosened a couple of my bottom teeth.

Two days later I went home with a brace glued to my teeth and two bandaged feet. I had been entered in the first road race of my life that weekend but, of course, I couldn't be there. Not only was I in a fair bit of pain but the bike was more than slightly second hand. I had not seen a bike damaged so badly before. The front wheel was pushed back into the engine. It was a write-off.

The mid '80s road race scene was fairly strong in New Zealand, and the 250cc and 600cc production classes were where you found all the rising young guns. The 250 bikes to ride were the Yamaha RZ250, Suzuki RG250, and Kawasaki KR250. The 600cc class was full of Yamaha RZ350s, Suzuki GSX550s, and Kawasaki GPZ600s. and both classes attracted the interest of New Zealand's bike distributors who were enjoying strong sales at the time. Since the 350 was a write-off, Ross and I decided to buy a second-hand RZ250, which was cheaper, and transplant the engine from the wrecked 350 into that. We would have a RZ350 to race and then sell, thus putting a positive spin on the crash. I was a Yamaha man, right down to my 'lucky' Yamaha underwear, so the RZ was the only choice for me.

The underpants were one of my racing lucky charms. There was a New Zealand sports clothing brand called Holeshot, and they made motocross jerseys and stuff like that. There was also a range of underpants to match the bike you rode, and mine were a white pair with red elastics and 'Yamaha' screen-printed on the backside. I always had good luck wearing these briefs, and I saved them just for race days, and then wore them until they lived up to their brand name. Once they were gone I didn't feel I had to replace them. Given the bad luck that was to come, perhaps I should have saved them for the World Superbike campaigns. Imagine Honda's top Superbike rider wearing 'Yamaha' on his backside! That would have sent HRC into a spin. The other lucky charm was my '111' numberplate. It started as my number back in junior motocross days, mostly because it was so easy to put on the bike. All you needed was three strips of insulation tape, and you were racing.

I was wearing both the number and the underpants when I lined up on the grid for my first road race, on something other than a motocross bike, at Manfield in August 1984. Underneath me was the rebuilt RZ350, ahead of me a sea of riders from the Victoria University Motorcycle Club from Wellington, arguably one of the most active in New Zealand when it comes to road racing. It was the Vic Club's winter series, and 17 years ago it was the domain of a certain Brian Bernard. Just like it still is today. Bernard beat me by almost a lap that first meeting. But I would get better every round of the series, closing the gap on him. It dropped to the length of a straight, then one corner, and soon his winning margin could be measured in seconds, then less than a second. Before the series ended, I was dicing with him.

I didn't know why I kept improving. It wasn't until later I learned to analyse my racing to find out how I could lift my performance. Every time racers get on motorbikes they tend to go as fast as they can go, and sometimes that involves falling off, sometimes it doesn't. The easiest way to go faster is to brake later. To get your lap times down, you brake several metres later, keep your same corner speed and you will be faster by quite a margin. Because of my motocross background, braking late came naturally. I never let anyone out-brake me in those early days, because I'd wait until whoever I was racing with to brake first before I'd touch my levers. It took a long time to learn that corner speed suffered as a result of braking too late. It wasn't any good for lap times, but it got me amongst the good guys where I could learn things. I am sure it brassed them all off to have this kid from Masterton slowing everybody down by out braking them, then cruising through the corner, but that's how I learnt my trade.

Riding on tar made me feel invincible. All the knowledge from motocross could now be applied to a motorcycle racing code with more traction. It made such a big difference coming from grass to tarseal. I thought I was bullet proof. I thought I could brake anywhere I liked on the road circuits and still pull up in time. But if I was getting faster without knowing why, I was also crashing without knowing why. I can remember getting my first set of new leathers and I crashed that day. I was going faster and faster, and then I crashed, flung over the high side, spat over the handlebars like a bullet from a gun. Maybe I went too fast, but I couldn't work it out because it happened so quickly. High sides are like that. You get flicked over the bars and the next thing you go whack on the ground, asking what did you do that was so wrong? Without the luxury of a slow-motion video replay, that question can be hard for a young racer to answer, and it's easy to get the enthusiasm for riding hard beaten out of you.

Not that it happened to me, for I had the honour of Gregory Motorcycles and Masterton to uphold. At the next national road race series, which the Vic Club's winter series was essentially practice for, we won the 1985 New Zealand 250cc Production Championship. It was the first of three such titles I'd win with Ross's help, and it was arguably the most enjoyable racing of my career. Everyone would take their holidays around the time of the South Island rounds of the series, and we'd leave a few staff to run the shop, load up the van, and hit the road. We could almost pretend this was the big time - staying in motels, and travelling from circuit to circuit like it was continental Europe. The tracks were great too. Manfield will always be my favourite, as its series of straights linked by tight corners suits my stop-go-stop-go riding style, but the Levels circuit near Timaru, and Teretonga, right at the South Island's southern end, were also tracks I always looked forward to racing on.

My Dad, Rex, took on the team management role. We would never miss out on a place in the paddock as Dad was always rushing everybody out of the motel at 7 am to get the best spot. He'd wake us all up with a cup of tea, and badger us until we got moving. Maybe somebody should have told him there would be plenty of spots left at 9 am. On the sleepy Sunday mornings, typical of New Zealand, we'd be driving down deserted roads to the track, while other teams were still sleeping in their motels and tents. I must admit we always had the best spots at Wanganui's Cemetery Circuit, where the pits were a bit more crowded than at a purpose-built road circuit. Dad used to set everything up the day before when we raced there. He always had a chillybin of food handy so no one went hungry. It was usually full of buckets of Kentucky Fried Chicken.

Soon our focus wasn't just the junior production classes, and, courtesy of Ross and Cushla, I had a stable of bikes to race - a new 250, the RZ350 and a RZ500. The NZ Yamaha distributor, Moller Yamaha had brought Michael Dowson and Richard Scott in for the Castrol 6-Hour for production bikes. They were to ride RZ500's prepared by Moller Yamaha. Ross had also bought a brand new RZ500, which was in the shop for sale. He took it along to the meeting as a spare. Michael Dowson ended up choosing the brand new bike over the Moller prepared bike. This bike had not turned a wheel. With half an hour to run in the race, Dowson crashed the brand new bike. So Ross said, "It's buggered now, so you might as well fix it up and race it in the open production." But the 500cc V4 wasn't my favourite bike. That honour would go to the first four-stroke I raced - a Yamaha FZ750. I loved that 750, as it was the first bike I rode with enough power to spin up the back wheel in the dry. The only real difference it made to my riding style after years of racing two-strokes was that it had engine braking, and shifting down for the corners would get the back end of the bike loose. When I watch replays on video, I'm always amused by World Superbike commentators who say: "So-and-so is backing the bike into the bends with the back brake". What's really happening is the downshifts going into the corner have broken the rear wheel away, and there's a bit of oversteer turning into the turn. The best way to race a four-stroke is to use very little, if any, back brake.

The Boxing Day racing at the Cemetery Circuit rated as New Zealand's most prestigious bike racing event, as it was shown live on TV all day, each racing class interlaced with horse racing at Auckland's Ellerslie racecourse. It always made spectacular viewing, as the circuit was a street event and as dangerous as hell. You had to cross railway lines and encounter white lines and pedestrian crossings and, if you got off-line, you would hit the kerbs. Many a racer's day at Wanganui has ended in the local accident and emergency ward.

With nothing in the way of hills or mountains to shelter Wanganui, the prevailing westerly winds would blow in fronts from the Tasman Sea, and a wet race was always on the cards. There's nothing like wet railway lines mid-corner to turn bikes into tank-slapping beasts. And nothing like a fiery crash into the hay-bales to keep a TV sports producer happy. It was called the Cemetery Circuit because it cut through the dead centre of town, literally right through Wanganui's cemetery. There was always a piss take from some of the local lads, who liked to fill a coffin with ice and beer, and dress up as undertakers to carry their macabre elongated chilly bin.

Despite the obvious danger, I always enjoyed riding at Wanganui. Especially if the heavens opened, as the shiny and slippery road circuit suddenly put my production bikes on equal terms with the hardcore race bikes. I'll never forget the day I beat Dr Roger Freeth there. It was one of the best rides of my career. He was on the mighty MacIntosh-Suzuki 1100 he used to dominate the New Zealand Formula One championship with. The ultra-light but highly rigid tube steel frame, built by Auckland's Ken MacIntosh, was a work of race craft that would have made Ducati take notice, and the engine pumped out heaps of horsepower. Freeth was on proper race wets, I was on a bog-stock Yamaha FZ750 wearing road tyres. We battled all through the last race - the 'run-what-you-brung', free-for-all that carried the biggest purse of the day. Roger wasn't going to let all the dough slip through his hands, blasting the more powerful MacIntosh past me on the straights, before I'd return the favour on the brakes. Leading onto the start-finish straight at Wanganui, there's a wicked left-hander over a railway overbridge. Not only do the bridge expansion joints unsettle the bike, the corner exit is way off-camber. I got a better drive than Roger heading for the chequered flag, and won the race by millimetres.

The icing on the cake was that this was one of the first occasions I could watch my racing on video afterwards. I had just made every TV viewer's Boxing Day, and enjoyed fame for the first time in my life.

The other big event on the New Zealand calendar, especially for those racing production bikes, was the Castrol 6-Hour endurance race held every November at Manfield. The 6-Hour and the Boxing Day races were great social events for all my mates from Masterton. I would race my butt off and they would get on the booze up in the stands. So we all enjoyed ourselves. I did happen to win the 6-Hour twice so they had something to celebrate. God knows how they made it home afterwards. Several years later I learnt that one friend's underage daughter ended up driving her father and uncle back to Masterton after the event. A one and half-hour drive for a 14-year-old unlicensed driver barely able to peer over the steering wheel must have been quite an ordeal.

The first 6-Hour win came on the faithful FZ750 in 1986. I had noticed that Rob Doran, a young gun from South Australia, was making a name for himself across the Tasman. So in 1985 I tracked him down and suggested he join our team for the 6-Hour. We proved unbeatable in our second attempt in 1986 and it was a relatively easy victory. The 750 made it so. It was a sweet handler, although it did have a lack of ground clearance, and we had worn through the exhaust pipes by the end of the race. In comparison, the FZR1000 I raced with Aussie Wayne Clarke the following year was a bucket of shit. The press had raved about the bike in their early reviews, and I'm sure the fans all thought the alloy-framed 1000 would be more competitive than the less glamorous steel tube framed 750, but the 1987 6-Hour win was much harder work.

I dropped the bike 45 minutes into the race, braking too hard for the hairpin, and losing the front. I was really angry with myself as I rode back to the pits for our mandatory post-crash check, but then I saw the Wellington Motorcycles GSX-R750 in the ditch, and felt a bit better. At least the FZR, with the twin-spar alloy frame protecting the engine, was more durable than the vulnerable Suzuki in a crash. The Wellington Motorcycles team lost four laps replacing a broken engine cover, while we were back out again straight away. Although Wellington M/C's Bob Toomey would record the fastest times of the race as he struggled to recover the lost laps, we still won by two laps from another GSX-R, with the Wellington bike finishing third. While these endurance race wins meant little offshore, they were huge in New Zealand at the time. All the bike distributors got involved every November at Manfield, believing that what won there that particular Sunday, would sell out the following Monday.

The New Zealand scene was very social, and on a Sunday evening when racing was over, there was either a barbecue at the track with a few beers, or at a local pub where everybody would congregate to collect their prize money. We were fierce competitors on the track, but when the racing was over, we were all mates again, despite some of the handlebar-banging that might have taken place earlier in the day. It was a bit like the rugby scene, really. There might be a bit of a punch-up on the field, a bit of niggling, but you'd leave all the arguments on the field of battle, and talk together that night as equals. The camaraderie was probably encouraged by New Zealand's isolation, and the huge hurdles facing anyone whose talent gave them the opportunity for success on the international scene.

I had several worthy rivals for success on the New Zealand championship scene. Most of all, Robert Holden was *the* man to beat during my time racing in New Zealand. He rode a stable of Wellington Motorcycles-prepared production Suzukis, and had an innovative F1 bike, which was called the "plastic fantastic". It featured a composite-kevlar monocoque frame made by Steve Roberts in Wanganui, and it was so competitive and ahead of its time the Australians banned it from their Swann Series. The Roberts bike was another example of Kiwi ingenuity, right up there with the Richard Pearse aeroplane that took to the air before the Wright Brothers, and our America's Cup winning yachts. Robert rode in all the production classes and seemed to have a good sponsorship package from Wellington Motorcycles. He had huge reserves of natural ability. He also had the advice and experience of workshop manager Steve Dundon, and he could often clean up in all classes. Tragically, Robert lost his life at the Isle of Man TT. I had talked with him the summer before, and he told me it was maybe his last trip to the island. Robert loved to race street circuits and was New Zealand's Joey Dunlop. I could not see him retiring in the near future because of his love of bikes. I have always regretted not being able to attend his funeral in New Zealand. His ashes were scattered at the Cemetery Circuit, where you'll now find a memorial to the man who won the most races there.

Dr Roger Freeth contended only the F1 class, where he and Robert often battled for the premier championship right down to the last corner of the last race of the last round. Roger taught astro-physics at an Auckland university, and applied his considerable intelligence to his racing. Everything he seemed to do, from bike preparation to his clinical passing manoeuvres, seemed deliberately, sometimes painstakingly, planned. Sadly, he too is no longer with us. He was killed at the Rally of Australia while navigating for Asia-Pacific Rally champion Possum Bourne, when their factory-supported Subaru hit a gum tree.

Bob Toomey was Robert Holden's team-mate at Wellington Motorcycles, and just as fast. He also broke into the big-time briefly in Australia, winning the 750cc class at their Castrol 6-Hour at his first attempt. However, a badly broken leg halted his efforts there, and he returned to New Zealand to be one of the top contenders in all classes. The international success that eluded Bob as a rider has come his way as a mechanic. He is currently the head technician for Kenny Roberts Jnr. in the factory Suzuki Grand Prix team.

Robbie Dean used to bash handlebars with Graeme Crosby and is still one of the hard men of the New Zealand racing landscape today. Age has only slightly slowed him down. In my Wanganui days, he was a rabid pit bull terrier on the street circuit. I remember watching Robbie when his bike would try to chuck him over the high side. In typical Robbie Dean fashion, he stayed on board, although the recovery was hardly pretty. No bike would dare chuck Robbie off.

Eddie Kattenberg started racing about the same time as Peter Blackwood and he was making a name for himself when I came on the scene. Eddie soon moved on to Australia to try to break into the big time, but struggled for many years. At the time of my hand injury in 1990 I left my trusty XB Falcon in Eddie's hands. He used it as a tow car for his racing. Things were tight and Eddie definitely put more preparation into his race bike than my poor old XB. Eddie was always in the middle of it all at the local prize givings and we had some good laughs.

Richard Scott was racing in Europe during the late 1980s and returned to do the major races of the Christmas season. He was a good gauge for younger riders to measure themselves against as he had made it into the Lucky Strike Yamaha 500 team managed by Kenny Roberts Snr. at the time. Scotty's New Zealand legacy was a lap record around Wanganui, set on a Honda NR500 triple, a record that stood for over 10 years.

Tony Rees was a major rival in the 250 production class and a good mate on the social scene. He was another ex-motocrosser using the 250 class as a stepping stone to greater things. He's the current New Zealand F1 champ, and making a bit of a name for himself in the Formula Xtreme series in Australia.

Brian Bernard was known for his long plaited hair. His was the first scalp I ever chased after because he kept leading the Vic Club's winter series events. He was the local king of the Manfield track, the first guy I had to beat to get anywhere. These days his racing is a bit easier, with support from Suzuki New Zealand.

Simon Crafar was just making an impact on the New Zealand scene as I was leaving for Australia. We later crossed paths, and swords, in the Malaysian Superbike championship. There, Simon rode the wheels off the OWO1 750 given him by the local Yamaha distributor. He seemed to follow, too closely at times, in my footsteps. He continued to show his face throughout my career. He suddenly became my team-mate at Castrol Honda in '95 when Doug Polen abruptly left after one year of his two-year contract. Simon even got to guest ride my Honda in 2000 while I was recovering from my operation.

Andrew Stroud is the most laid-back motorcycle racer you will ever meet. Yet his apparent sleepiness belied his speed. He probably pushed me harder than anyone else in the 250 production class in my early years. I was pleased to see he got the Super Angel ride in '89. Simon Crafar also joined the Super Angel team for the Suzuka 8-Hour and then stayed on for the rest of the year, probably to Andrew's detriment as he was now sharing his equipment and had another person to beat. I remember a story while sharing the same pit as Andrew. I was trying to go out for a practice session, but couldn't find my gloves. It wasn't until Andrew came back in and took off his helmet and gloves that I found them, rather sweaty and used. When I questioned him he did admit, "I thought they were a bit small". Only then did he notice they were a different colour and brand to his. He was so laid-back the Britten motorcycle team once found him asleep in the van just minutes before a race. Yet once on the track he was fast and smooth. A great guy, his biggest opportunity for recognition so far has come from his rides on the Britten bikes, in the Battle of the Twins support class at the Daytona 200. Andrew has also won the New Zealand F1 title for Britten motorcycles.

Norris Farrow competed mainly in the open class on a MacIntosh-Suzuki similar to Freeth's and was finishing racing just as I was starting. However, years later he ended up being my chief mechanic at Castrol Honda, and was able to assess my feedback from a rider's as well as from a mechanic's perspective.

Jason McEwen was a Palmerston North lad who was starting to go quite strongly about the same time as me, but he had a big crash at the Cemetery Circuit which slowed him up for a couple of years. He was always very fast but never broke into overseas racing properly. He finally broke Scotty's Wanganui record on one of John Britten's bikes. The fans nicknamed Jason "the hippie" for his long hair and attitude.

Brent Jones made the New Zealand Formula Two class his playground; racing proper TZ Yamaha 250 Grand Prix bikes against modified 600cc four-stroke sportsbikes. He also did some GPs, often popping up on the grid of the Malaysian rounds. He was one of several good South Island riders at the time, along with Rob Lewis and the Ramage brothers - Grant and Allan. Brent's father, Craig, came to Japan with me in '88 to try to sort out the Super Angel TZ250 I was supposed to race alongside a Bimota YB4 Superbike. However, the team decided to concentrate on the Bimota, and unfortunately it was a wasted three to four weeks for Craig.

Glenn Williams returned to New Zealand often to do the summer series. He was making a name for himself in England at the time, but would return to fly the Kawasaki flag in the New Zealand season. He was always their best chance for 6-Hour success, and a spectacular rider on the street circuits, where the crowd loved his big wheelies.

To readers with an international perspective, some of these names will be familiar, some will not. Yet all of them deserved international success, all had the skill and the talent to operate at the highest levels of the sport. The fact that just a few did is testimony to the hurdles facing New Zealand riders. It's tougher for Kiwi racers to make it than those from any other nation with a motorcycle culture. The country has just three and a half million people, and if you tip the globe so New Zealand is in the centre, you'll see just Australia and half a hemisphere of deep blue sea. Not only does the New Zealand motorcycle market pale to insignificance in comparison with other countries, making it hard to justify places for Kiwi riders in international teams, but motorcycle racing there has the added disadvantage of a low profile. You won't find pages of motorcycle racing news in New Zealand newspapers like you will in Spain and Italy. And you won't find the factories saying we must select a rider from New Zealand to race for us, because our sales are so important there. But perhaps the biggest hurdle is the geographic isolation, and the way it extends the career path of a New Zealand racer determined to make the big time internationally. For an American rider, that path is clear - win the national championship, then take on the world. Ditto for Italian, French, German, and British riders. But New Zealand riders have no such career path.

Because of the success of Wayne Gardner and Mick Doohan, the Australians need no introduction however. For New Zealanders, the first step to Europe is to have success in New Zealand. Then the next stage is to go over to Australia and have success there. Then, hopefully, make the move to Europe. Therefore, Australians are already one step ahead of New Zealand riders. I recognise, and am thankful for, the path that Australia gave to me. If it wasn't for Peter Doyle and Kawasaki Australia my career would never have taken off.

So I decided the only way to break through internationally was to island-hop. Once I reached Australia I knew I needed to win every championship they threw at me, from the Pan Pacific to the Australian Superbike Championships. Hopefully I would attract the attention of overseas teams and sponsors. I thought that if I turned up in Europe with just about every Asia-Pacific regional championship on my CV, the teams might just overlook where I came from. I'd take on Malaysia, Japan, and anywhere else on either side of the Pacific Ocean where they raced motorcycles. But first I had to win in Australia.

four

A Kiwi: Eats Roots and Leaves

The New Zealand economy revolves around the export of primary products. Things like meat, wool, timber, apples, and... people. The country's isolation fill its sons and daughters with an urge to see the rest of the world, and one of its most well known exports is professional sportspeople. In New Zealand, there are two qualifications every teenager aspires to - UE or University Entrance, and OE - Overseas Experience. For many it's just a temporary thing - chuck on a backpack, fly to London, and hitchhike back again. But those wanting to reach the very top quickly find that they're big fish swimming inside New Zealand's little goldfish bowl. Most of our best film directors live in Hollywood along with our actors, our musicians quickly become honorary Australians, and our sportspeople start playing for other teams. With an island nation of just over three and a half million people, busting out is like leaving a middle-sized city for the rest of the world.

Looking back, I certainly took a long time to reach Europe. But it wasn't like I had any choice. I just took the opportunities that were open to me as financing my own way to Europe was an impossibility. These opportunities led me to the World Superbike Championship. Eventually. I arrived late on that scene because of all the zigzags I took getting there. Perhaps the young Kiwis following me are doing the right thing by taking a more direct route. They're doing what we call "keeping your eyes on the ball" in a rugby-mad country. They're turning down offers to perform in the many backwater championships that dot the Pacific Rim, and paying their own way to swim with the big fish in the middle of the stream. CART Indycar star Scott Dixon paid his dues in Indy Lights and got himself noticed right away. World 250cc Motocross Championship contender Josh Coppins turned down comfortable rides in Australia so he could keep on contesting the most competitive motocross championship in the world, while paying his own way.

I talked to Josh when he was about 15, and stepping up to the senior ranks for the first time. He was visiting the Burkhart boys - Luke and Jonathan - who were destined to become Masterton's next motorsport guns. Their father heard I was in town, and asked me to go out to talk to the boys at their practice track. I didn't really know what to say, but maybe Josh took something on board from that pep talk. I told him I spent a lot of time winning this championship and winning that race, but that you are only as good as those you compete against. Trying the harder road means competing against tougher riders, and no one knows how good they are until they take on the world's best. Now Josh is one of the world's best, and a factory rider for Suzuki at age 22.

Age is important in this business, especially when emerging from little old New Zealand. I remember telling a newspaper reporter there that if I didn't get my big break by 27, I might as well not bother. I was 23 at the time, and things were starting to look good. My first race on a racetrack outside New Zealand was in 1986 when I was 20, and those three years in between were a long tough fight to be recognised.

It started when Rob Doran, my riding partner in the 1985 New Zealand Six-Hour, offered me accommodation at his flat – more an oversized cupboard – in Sydney. He said I should come to Australia in 1986 and compete in the 250 Production series. I went to live with him and his girlfriend, and a Kiwi mechanic - Trevor Love. I emptied my bank accounts in New Zealand, flew across the Tasman Sea, and spent my entire life savings on a new RZ250 for the 250 Production class.

It wasn't as though I had made up my mind to be a professional motorcycle racer. I went to Australia to make a name for myself, and hopefully attract a sponsor. But I didn't have the confidence to go knocking on people's doors. I just hoped that if I could defeat better-supported riders with my limited budget, the doors would automatically open for me.

I got a pretty good deal on the RZ250 from Rob's sponsor, but it took all the money I had. I didn't have anything left to register the bike or insure it. I rode it around Sydney with some old number plate on it, trying to run it in. One Sunday afternoon I decided to ride out to Amaroo Park and watch a club day. On the way home I was getting into it and sneaked past a couple of cars on double yellow lines. Soon after, I was being pulled over by the New South Wales police. They checked on the computer as to who owned the bike via the number plate. It came back as a

KR250, so all of a sudden they were trying to charge me for stealing a motorbike because it wasn't a KR at all. They said they had to take me to the police station to make a statement, and I would have to prove that I owned the bike. I convinced them to let me push my bike up someone's driveway as I knew if it was left on the side of the road it would be stolen. I rang Rob to bring me the paperwork and bail me out as the owner of the unregistered bike. He bought the van, collected me from the police station, loaded up the bike and we returned to the flat. A month later, I had to appear in court and plead guilty to riding an unregistered, uninsured, motorbike and passing on double yellows. The penalty was A$500 and a couple of hours in the local lock up. My one and only time behind bars.

It all ended in poverty. Rob loaned me his van to take the bike to the races, after I promised to give it a tune-up, but I only had the resources to do four races. The last race I entered was in Surfers Paradise, and although I finished second, my money had run out. The promise was there for all to see. The only guy who beat me that day was some up-and-comer called Mick Doohan. I hadn't a clue who he was at the time, but I envied his support. He had a sponsor who would become his personal manager throughout his racing career. I worked on my own bike that weekend, using just the tool kit the bike came with. After the race, I sold the RZ and spent the money on an air ticket back home. I had spent six months in Australia, and got only four races because I didn't know my way around. It was a huge learning curve.

Some people might think I've got a chip on my shoulder about being born in New Zealand. Don't get me wrong; it's a great country, especially if you love the outdoors. It's just not so great if you happen to be trying to break through internationally in a professional sport with the amount of investment and commitment that motorcycle racing requires. Look at the career path of Max Biaggi. He wins an Italian national championship, then a European championship, then the next year he's racing in the Grand Prix. In three years, he goes from paying his own way to a full factory ride. All because he was born in the right place. European guys could take the elevator to success, where I had to scramble up 20 flights of stairs.

Back in New Zealand, the racing wasn't as tough. I had the support of my local sponsors and could enjoy the comforts of home. Ross quickly got me aboard a TZR250 Yamaha for the 250cc production championship, and we cut the opposition to ribbons. The TZR was the successor to the RZ250 I raced across the Tasman, and it was the bike to be on if you wanted to win the championship in the 1986/87 New Zealand season. I won 21 races from 22 starts on my 'trusty' TZR.

The one race I did not win was the 1986 Champion Sparkplugs 2-Hour at Manfield. That day I was just beaten by Ian 'Buster' Saunders, a little Aussie battler if ever there was one. Buster rode the wheels off anything. He had earned his nickname a year or two before when racing a Kawasaki 900. Every ride he would evidently 'bust' a gearbox. He rode the 2-Hour for a South Island team who took a liberal view of the production class rules. My bike was 'fairly' close to stock and he was smoking me down the straights. It was a great race as we battled for the full two hours.

But perhaps the best thing that happened on my return home in October 1986 was meeting Megan, my partner of the past 15 years, and wife for five. Perhaps it was what happened to my parents that kept me from taking her to the altar earlier. She was flatting with a good friend of mine in Masterton, and when I came around for a visit, we met for the first time. We hit it off straight away. Like all good relationships, it started with a physical attraction, but unlike the girlfriends I had met in the past, she wasn't hard work. We immediately felt comfortable in each other's company. Before Megan, none of my girlfriends had lasted more than four weeks. I wanted to race bikes, have fun, and if a partner could fit into that then it was cool, but if they couldn't I never regarded it as any great loss. It wasn't that they were always demanding time and effort, but they had to compete with my commitment to motorcycle racing. When we first met Megan probably thought it was something I'd grow out of, but she obviously decided to humour me in the meantime, given what she had to put up with in our early days together. I could see I was on the verge of a break-through, and I had complete faith in my ability as a rider. The potential probably wasn't as obvious to her, and she definitely took a gamble when deciding to include me in her life. She probably thought: "He won't always be throwing his money away racing bikes. Sooner or later, he'll move out of his father's house, get a flat, and we'll settle down together". Little did she know at the time, that it would mean waiting over a decade before we'd finally settle permanently into an apartment in Monaco.

We were both young and Megan enjoyed the independence of her new relationship. As with past girlfriends I didn't want to compromise. Through our first summer together, Dad would wake me up with a cup of tea at 7.30, and I'd be at work at 8.00 am. Lunch times were spent at Nana Slight's, a 30-minute break shared with my father and uncle Bernie.

Then I'd work until 5.30, go home for a run past Megan's new flat, and then have dinner, before returning to the shop to work on my race bikes. At 10.30, I'd stop, and go to see Megan for a bit before returning home to Dad's. It was all part of the time and effort that every successful motorcycle racer puts in, and the glue must have been strong to hold Megan and me together.

Success on my home tracks made me more determined than ever to break out of the New Zealand straitjacket. I remember asking my father what he thought I should do. The 1986 trip to Australia had felt like a bit of a waste of time and money. Although looking back, finishing second to Mick Doohan in a field full of young Aussie talent wasn't something to be ashamed off. Dad suggested that instead of buying a bike over there, I should ship the TZR over, and race it. That way, I could leave the bike in Australia, and instead of twiddling my thumbs between races, fly back to New Zealand to work.

It was the right formula. For the 1987 season, Australia participated in something called the Yamaha Cup. It was a one-make series intended to foster young talent. The participating countries would send the winner of their national series to an international final in Europe. Because the distribution of Yamaha bikes in New Zealand was handled by a private company - Moller Yamaha - New Zealand wasn't involved, but I thought I could gatecrash the Aussie series. The Cup races were fierce battles, and although I got good results, the officials didn't like this upstart Kiwi beating their young guns. They told me my points wouldn't be counted, and that if I won the series I wouldn't get the trip to Europe, as I wasn't a citizen of their country. Not that I was gutted. I actually thought it was a compliment at the time, a real boost to my ego. I felt flattered they considered me a threat. It was the first time people in the paddock were scared of me.

But it wouldn't be the first time my country of origin affected me. Winning races in Australia got me noticed, and soon teams were offering me rides. First Bob Brown noticed my talents; he offered me a ride on his Ducati F2 at Winton Raceway where I was doing not so badly until the clutch fell apart. Then I rode with Robert Holden for the Action Suzuki team in the '87 Australian Castrol Six-Hour. We rode a GSX-R750 against 1000cc Yamahas and Hondas, and 900cc Kawasakis. Australia had a 1000cc capacity limit for production bike races, and the GSX-R1100 wasn't allowed to compete. It wasn't to be the last time I would have to race bigger bikes with a 750cc four-cylinder. Robert and I finished fourth in the Aussie Castrol 6-Hour, the first 750 to take the chequered flag.

At that Oran Park endurance race, we also made motorcycle racing history. It wasn't for our 750cc class victory, but for what happened mid-race. The race was broadcast live on Australian TV, and the producers had fitted out my helmet with a microphone and speakers so the commentators could cross live for some on-bike mid-race comment. I was flicking through the flip-flops at Oran Park, and had the bike sideways, when the producer decided it was a good time for Wil Hagon to talk to me. I was struggling to keep control, when his voice suddenly erupted in my ears at maximum volume. The flip-flops are a crucial part of the Oran Park circuit, and they require maximum concentration. Because of Oran Park's slightly hilly nature, the apexes of the flip-flops are blind, and if you get off-line there, you're either onto the grass on one side of the track, or smashing your bike and body into a concrete wall on the other. I screamed back at Hagon and clear into millions of homes across Australia that day, and it was the first, and last time any TV coverage of bike racing included heat-of-battle comment from a competitor.

It was also the first time I chatted to Rob Phillis, who would later become one of my closest friends. Rob couldn't ride that day, and as an absolute legend of the Aussie scene, had been asked to help with the commentary. He quickly cut short the chatter with Hagon, saying, "We can see you're a bit busy right now Aaron, how about we get together for a beer after the race". We did, and celebrated the 750 class win. Also that night I can remember Rob making a few bob with his "famous party trick" which I was to see for the first time, but unfortunately not the last.

The Bob Brown Ducati and Action Suzuki rides were the first time I raced anything other than Yamaha. Loyalty is something that's bred into me, and it's a value I cherish, but there was no Yamaha ride on offer to me at the time. My association with Yamaha started because my father Rex bought a 50cc scooter from Ross Gregory, and it was Ross who lived across the road, and came over to show me how to clean Uncle Dave's GT80MX. Had Dad bought a Honda, my early allegiance would have been to the H-brand. It's hard to turn down a free ride when you're a young racer spending every last cent on furthering your career.

In those days, the Australian race season would climax with the Swann Series - a three-round championship where all the stars of the nation would return to race. That year Mal Campbell and Rob Scolyer rode the NR750 Hondas - special oval-piston prototype F1 bikes. To compete, the Marlboro Yamaha Team rode their Superbikes with 1000cc engines.

Rob Phillis did not ride the Kawasaki as they had nothing fast enough to compete. Robert Holden rode his Action Suzuki Superbike, and I battled in the middle of the field with the likes of Anders Anderson and others on F1 spec bikes on the infamous Bob Brown Ducati.

It would be another five or six years before Ducati really emerged on the Superbike scene, but Bob Brown was an Australian Seventh Day Adventist who built a fire-breathing 900cc weapon out of a 600cc Formula Two bike. Bob's greatest handicap in bike racing was that he always gave Saturday over to his spiritual pursuits, while his greatest assets were his bike and his tuning skill. It was his Ducati that launched the career of Kevin Magee, who went on to become a factory 500 rider in the Kenny Roberts-led Lucky Strike.

With the quality of the Swann series grid, it didn't really help to have a bike and team that missed Saturday's practice sessions until I persuaded Bob to let a mechanic bring the bike earlier. At the first rounds, I'd hitch a ride to the tracks with Robert Holden and the Action Suzuki crew, then wait impatiently for Bob and the Ducati to show up. Saturday would be spent watching all the other riders dial in their bikes and get the first choice of the tyres.

The Bob Brown rides did get me noticed, and gave me confidence that I could compete at the world level. Most races I'd been dicing with Anders Andersson, the Swedish Superbike champion and Suzuki's top contender in the World Formula One Championship. Suddenly the phone started ringing. First call was from Yamaha Australia. Kevin Magee was off to Europe, and they needed a replacement. However there was an Australian also up for the ride. Mick Doohan wanted to return from

Japan, where he had been riding in the Japanese F1 Championship for the Super Angel team. He got the ride, the Aussie distributor favouring the locally born rider. A career path that would eventually lead Doohan to become the most successful two-stroke rider in the history of 500cc Grand Prix suddenly closed its doors on me.

But there's an old saying that when one door closes, another door opens. Doohan's departure left a vacancy at Super Angel, and the team owner, Mr Morinaga, was the next to call, complete with an interpreter. The Super Angel ride seemed to offer so much. There were factory bikes from Yamaha, and the chance to perform in front of the most powerful people in the motorcycle world. Morinaga too was an interesting guy. He owned a large Yamaha dealership in Japan, yet he wasn't your typical Japanese businessman. He wasn't over-polite, and he seemed to have a more global view of the world. He didn't seem to care that his rider was not Japanese. In fact, I think it suited him to have a foreigner to attract attention, as long as they did the business come race day.

Despite the name, the Super Angel ride turned out to be hell. The Yamaha factory connection dried up as soon as I arrived. Evidently, the factory had just given Morinaga the machines while he set up his team around Doohan as a reward for being a top selling Yamaha outlet that year. Morinaga had also promised me a TZ250 GP bike to ride, as well as a Bimota YB4 Superbike with a Yamaha 750cc engine. I thought the TZ would be my best opportunity to break into the Grand Prix world, and Morinaga had two of each bike to run in the 250 and Formula One Japanese championships respectively. Money was obviously no problem for Morinaga, but I felt he lacked kindness and understanding. He might have put me up in a five-star hotel for months, but I felt like his pet in a gilded cage. Every day I had to go to the motorcycle shop. He'd call by and pick me up at 9.00 am, and drop me off on the way home at 7.00 pm. There was nothing for me to do there. I couldn't work on the bikes, as the mechanics felt that was their responsibility, and they didn't want a foreigner messing around with them. I felt I was a display. If he could have put me in a glass cage with a little sign saying "Mr Morinaga's pet foreign rider" I'm sure he would have. Instead, I'd struggle to communicate with his customers, drink hundreds of cups of coffee, and wonder when this nightmare would end. I was lonely, and in complete culture shock. I hated Japanese food at the time, although I love it now. That just shows the negative space I was in. I missed Megan, and missed the rest of my family. I even missed Masterton.

I was racing the TZ in the Japanese 250cc Grand Prix, and 22 laps into the 26-lap race, it seized. The engine locked up so suddenly, I couldn't get the clutch in soon enough to prevent the bike tossing me over the bars. It happened in one of the fastest corners of the Suzuka circuit (130R), and suddenly I'm flying through the air at 230 km/h. I smashed my left little finger on landing. Yet at the time it felt like the best thing that ever happened to me. I had the excuse I needed to go home. Go home to Megan, my family, and the cold apple pies at my favourite bakery in Masterton.

Every day back home, Morinaga would ring to ask when I'd be coming back again. I put him off, telling him about the physiotherapy I was receiving in New Zealand I couldn't get back in Japan. When I returned, I bought along the best two-stroke mechanic I knew - Brent Jones' father Craig. I thought he'd soon get the TZ flying, as it was obvious the Super

Angel bikes weren't the fastest Yamahas in the field. He sat on his spanners for three weeks before Morinaga told us Super Angel would concentrate solely on Superbikes from now on. The disappointment overwhelmed us, and I suspect Morinaga made that call because the Japanese mechanics felt some loss of face with the sudden appearance of Craig in their midst.

It all became worthwhile when the world series of various championships visited Japan. When the 1988 World Formula One championship came calling at Sugo, I bought the Bimota home in 11th place. It wasn't a bad finish for a bike obviously down on speed compared with the rest of the field. But it was the World Superbike round at Sugo that would finally earn my ticket to a factory ride.

You might think I hate Sugo, considering the World Superbike Championships I've lost there. But I love the place. It's the Michelin tyres I would later ride on that couldn't come to grips with my favourite Japanese race track. When the World Superbike circus set up camp there in 1988, I rode the wheels off the Bimota for a seventh place finish, right behind Rob Phillis on the Team Kawasaki Australia Superbike. Peter Doyle led the TKA team, and it was being groomed as the premier Kawasaki team for the world champs. They had access to the best Kawasaki had to offer, yet here I was, giving Rob the hurry-up with a privateer Bimota. Peter was looking for another rider to team up with Rob. He offered me a ride in the coming Swann series, and said that if my results were good, it would lead to a contract to race in the Australian Superbike Championship. When I bought the Kawasaki GPX750 home in fifth and sixth at Oran Park, and sixth at Phillip Island, it sealed the deal.

Signing the contract with Kawasaki Australia was the first confirmation that I had made it. I was now earning a living totally from racing motorcycles. I was a fully paid professional rider at last. It was beginning to feel like the big time.

With financial security, came independence. I had lived with my father until getting my contract with Kawasaki. I had always been happy with the situation and it allowed me to save a lot of my money to go racing. Instead of rent, Dad and I had an agreement for me to pay off certain hire purchase products. I thought the house needed a video so that was my first rental payment. With the contract to race in Australia, suddenly the ties of home weren't so hard to cut. Megan and I moved to Albury/ Wondonga - a town with two names because of its position on the New South Wales/Victoria border.

We rented a brand new apartment, bought an XB Falcon and settled in, near the Phillis family. Rob's mother-in-law Glenda rallied around and lent us furniture. We lived with what we needed, mattress on the floor, tiny black and white TV, no luxuries but could not have been happier. A shopping expedition like we had never had before saw us fill the boot of the Falcon with gadgets and necessities for the apartment. It was like Christmas. We were like kids with new toys.

My training habits were now starting to change. I would do my usual thirty minute run every day but Rob's influence started to rub off on me. In the winter we would trail ride a couple of times a week and as soon as the water would start to get warm we would jet ski every other day. I bought a KX250 dirt bike from Kawasaki to train on and was very lucky to have Rob provide me with a jet ski. More often than not, he supplied the fuel as well.

If Kawasaki didn't fly us to race meetings, Rob and I would drive there together in his new Nissan Patrol. Rob always made me drive as I always quickly fell asleep if in the passenger seat. The roads are so straight and boring in Australia, the only way Rob could get a conversation out of me was to hand over the wheel. Sometimes I wondered why I accepted, as he would then tell me how to drive, nagging like an old woman to watch my speed and to slow down for corners. Yet he was a different man when it came to cars other than his own.

The West Australian round of the championship was too far to drive, so Rob and I flew in, and collected our team rental car, a hapless Ford Falcon wagon at the airport. Everybody had a go at that poor car that weekend. It somehow lost the bumper while double jumping the sand dunes near the Wanaroo circuit. We cable-tied it back on. Then Rob did a reverse to first shift with the thing going backwards. There was a large bang and the Falcon suddenly had no drive. We drove to the airport with only third and reverse gear, the car gliding around left corners as either the rallycross in the dunes, or Rob's shift-on-the-fly, had broken the axle. Rob had to drop the keys off before catching a flight. A couple of weeks later he was sent a bill for $A6000. Carol, his wife, wanted to kill him.

The scene was typical of Aussie bloke behaviour. One Aussie bloke was Reg O'Rourke, a mechanic, who, like Peter, never backed away from a brawl. I had heard plenty of stories about Reg, and one night Peter set me up a beauty. He said: "Go over and ask Reg how his sister's ballet dancing lessons are going". So I thought I might as well go along with their game, and went up and asked, "Reg, how are your sister's ballet dancing lessons going?" Reg's face dropped, his eyes blazed with anger, and he paused for a few seconds before replying, "My sister is in a wheel chair, asshole".

He then proceeded to take his false teeth out, which I knew from stories he always did before attacking. I knew I was in deep shit. A few more seconds later, Reg and Peter both burst out laughing as they knew they had scared the shit out of me. From that time on, Reg and I became great mates, and there was many a time I would have to hang onto his false teeth while he sorted out the bouncers or the dick heads.

Bouncers? I was the getaway car driver in Adelaide, while Reg and Peter sorted out the six bouncers at the casino. Things were starting to get out of hand and I noticed that there had been a call to the police so I was outside with the rental car running. Reg took his last few swings while being thrown out the door, and we took off to avoid any altercation with the South Australian law. Once again, I had Reg's teeth in my top pocket.

My first Australian Superbike Championship race for the team was at Symmons Plains in Tasmania - Honda stalwart Mal Campbell's home track. Although I didn't beat Mal, it was a good start, and I came second to Campbell in the first race, and third behind Mal and Rob in the second. World-class riders like Rob Phillis and Mal Campbell were the local racing benchmarks, and the men you had to beat on the day for any chance at the title. My first race win came on the same weekend as we were having fun in the rental car, at Wanaroo, Perth. I could not believe that finally I had won a race, during my first year with the team; such was the heat of the competition. I beat Peter Goddard to the line, while Rob finished third, followed by Michael Dowson and Mal. I had a first place trophy to take home. Earlier that day Peter gave me the factory F1 bike to ride in the 1000cc class and I won both those races too. I went on to finish third in the Australian Superbike Championship behind the two great long-time rivals for the title - Campbell and Phillis.

Now that I was associated with Kawasaki, I was being flown up to Japan for several different races and tests. This experience of Japan was very different from the year before, and I began to love Japan and its people. That year I rode a factory Kawasaki F1 bike, the new Superbike, and an F3 bike, which was heaps of fun - a ZXR400 that would rev to the moon. I also started testing the experimental Kawasaki 250cc Grand Prix machine, code named the XO9. Kawasaki tried all sorts of engine configurations for the 250, without a lot of success. I spent the next couple of years helping with development and raced it twice. Once at Sugo, Japan in early 1990, and then at Daytona in 1992. At Daytona it seized, and I got knocked unconscious. I was happy to part ways with the X09 as I thought I had bigger fish to fry at the time.

I was hopeful of great things to come in 1990. Rob would concentrate on the World Superbike Championship and Peter wanted me to fly the Kawasaki flag solo in Australia. Obviously I had done enough to make him feel confident I could win the championship for the team. Towards the end of 1989, I also competed in three World Superbike rounds. At Sugo, I finished in the top 10, at Oran Park, Australia, I was up to the top 5, and then at the last round at Manfield, New Zealand, I gained my first podium finish with a second to Terry Rymer in the rain. This was followed by a DNF in the second race, but I did set a new lap record at my home track - a 1.08.17 lap.

The Kawasaki Australia ride wasn't the only option on the table. I became embroiled in the politics around the 500cc World Championship in faraway Europe. Marlboro was threatening to take its sponsorship away from Giacomo Agostini's team and give it to Kenny Roberts. Ago tried to keep it , saying he might be able to persuade Suzuki superstar Kevin Schwantz to switch to his camp. Marlboro said if he could pull that one off they'd keep investing in his team. Schwantz was the most spectacular 500 rider of the time, a sure-fire ticket to plenty of media coverage, and best mobile billboard on two wheels. Ago asked me to come to Italy, and negotiate a ride as second rider to Schwantz in his Yamaha team. The deal was conditional on him securing Kevin. I raided my bank account for the airfare, and jumped on a plane to Italy, hopeful all my dreams were about to come true. Little did I know, while I was somewhere in the air over the Indian Ocean, Kevin was renewing his contract with Suzuki in Japan. Marlboro's millions would go to Kenny Roberts that coming 500 season. Ago, the great racer of the 1960s and '70s, was suddenly left out in the cold. With Marlboro's money went the ability to sign anyone, and Yamaha's fastest race bikes followed that vast sum.

Peter Doyle was miffed that I'd suddenly gone off to see Ago in the midst of the season. My Australian Superbike results suffered the following weekend after the long pointless flight. I finished the season with a fourth and a third. The 1989 Aussie Superbike Championship was the last chance for the old Aaron Slight - the 23-year-old who went fast without really knowing why. He would disappear in a horrific crash at Suzuka in 1990. But a stronger, smarter racer would emerge from the hospital bed.

five

Dealt a Cruel Hand

The 1990 season started well enough for me, but it soon all turned to custard. I came out with all guns blazing in the opening round of the Australian Superbike Championship, determined to be more aggressive than the previous year. The main opposition was a trio of Honda V4s ridden by the wily veteran Mal Campbell, and young lions Scott Doohan and Daryl Beattie. Then there was Peter Goddard on the Yamaha Australia superbike, partnered by the win-or-crash-trying Rene Bongers. With Rob concentrating on the World Series, I was the solitary green machine in a sea of red and white bikes on the Australian tracks.

Mal opened the series with a double victory at Baskerville, Tasmania. He also scored another double victory in the second round at Phillip Island near Melbourne, but this time by fractions of seconds. Mal beat me by 0.03 seconds in the first race and by 0.18 in the second. I felt confident, and losing both races at the Island on the last lap really brassed me off. Still, I had proved to myself, and the team, that I had the speed to win. There was no way Mal was going to beat me at the third round at Mallala in South Australia, and I took maximum points by winning both races. The second South Australian race was one of my closest ever. Mallala is tough on brakes, and I had problems with the front discs warping in the first race. I got a good start in the second, pulled a lead, then went easy on the brakes, but they still warped with seven laps to run. I couldn't brake all the way to the apex, as the juddering would upset the bike's steering when I tipped it into the bends. This allowed Goddard to catch up, and then pass, so I hung onto his tail, saving everything for the last three laps. I then pulled the pin, setting the fastest lap of the meeting on lap 23, but Goddard out-braked me on the last lap at the hairpin before the final esses. I'd passed him with the back wheel in the air at the same place the lap previous, but this time he waited a good couple of metres after I braked before throwing on the anchors, clipping me as he went past. He must have thought he had the race won at this point, but I stuffed the Kawasaki up the inside at the first of the esses, and snatched the racing line away by rubbing my front forks on his knee. I won by half a wheel, running him out wide on the final corner, with the crowd going wild. Goddard and I had banged into each other in each of the last three corners. There were tyre marks all over the legs of our leathers.

That double lifted me to third place in the championship, and after the fourth round in Perth, I was second to Mal Campbell when Goddard failed to fire. With two rounds of the championship to go, I was 23 points behind Campbell, and with 80 points still up for grabs, I was looking forward to taking him to the wire for the title. Then there were the World Superbike rounds Peter had entered me in after the Aussie championship. I had set a new lap record at my Manfield home track the year before, and was looking forward to lowering it further with the better performing bike I was riding in 1990. Before the Mallala wins, I had also spent the weekend in Japan testing the top-secret X09 GP250 bike again, and there was the possibility of riding in selected 250cc Grand Prixs. First I had to fly to Japan to do the Suzuka 200 km endurance race for Formula One bikes. It was to be practice for an 8-Hour effort later that year, with Michael Dowson booked as my riding partner. What started as relatively harmless practice nearly ended my career.

It was a Thursday afternoon at Suzuka, and I was testing the new Kawasaki Formula One bike. Although it shared the same ZXR750 genes as the superbike, it was one of the fastest four-stroke racing bikes in the world at the time. The best machine Kawasaki Heavy Industries could build. It was probably the last run of the day and we were rushing to get another last minute test done before the track closed. The Americans riding for the Muzzy Kawasaki team had already packed up for the day and they were on an early flight back to the U.S.A. for a local race. Doug Chandler and Scott Russell were Muzzy's riders and they had flown in for couple of days testing and would return for the 8-Hour. I was to race the 200km race that weekend as well and all Kawasaki's hopes were riding on me. The previous days of testing were the first time I had met Scott Russell, who would later become a close friend. Doug was a friendly guy who chewed tobacco. Scott was a bit more reserved and seemed to keep to himself, as he was full of confidence and was out to prove himself to everybody.

The crash wasn't particularly spectacular, but it produced the most destructive moment of my life. People might find this difficult to understand, as most would expect that the operation I had to remove the blood clot in my brain 10 years later would easily outweigh any other trauma I 'd had to overcome previously.

Just prior to having my stroke, I was sick for a long time without knowing why. It was such a huge relief to discover that I really was sick rather than crazy. I finally relaxed for the first time in months, secure in the knowledge that there was something physically wrong with me. I had already achieved so much by the time of my stroke. The most important thing at that point was to survive. With the Suzuka crash, my life wasn't in any danger, but there was a very real possibility of never riding again. It might sound strange, but I feared that fate worse than death. There was so much more unfinished business in 1990, and it looked like I might lose the use of my right hand.

I've replayed the crash over and over in my head. It was the sort of accident most bike racers would simply walk away from, return to pits, hop on the spare bike, and get on with finding the right set-up while the mechanics straightened the crashed bike out. It's odd how sometimes the smaller scale accidents are the most damaging. Mine was a second gear slide off the low side. For motorcycle racers there are two types of crash - 'low sides' and 'high sides'. A low side is when you lose the front wheel, the bike simply falls over, and you part company from the lower side of the seat. A low side is usually a non-event compared to losing the back wheel, trying to save it and getting pitched over the handlebars. We call these crashes high sides because you're chucked violently over the high side of the bike. The scars on my hands and forearms are proof that a low side crash can be equally dangerous - life-long souvenirs of Suzuka 1990.

Unfortunately I have a habit of holding onto the handlebars when I crash, a hangover from my motocross days. I wait until the last possible moment to let go as I may still have a chance to save it. It's typical of my confidence in my riding skill, and there have been plenty of times when the bike has slid out, gripped again, bucked me into the air like I'm in a rodeo, and I've managed to keep it on the track.

But there was no saving this crash. Part of our testing included trying different sized wheels - three and three quarter or three and a half inch rims. I went out on the bike after one of these changes was made, and I'm sure the wrong rim had been fitted by mistake - a narrower one than what I'd asked for. I was hard on the gas on the exit of the last bend - the infamous Suzuka chicane where Senna and Prost had their collision - as I started my first fast lap with the new set-up. The bike wheelied, which is nothing unusual when cracking open the throttle of a big powerful motorcycle in a low gear. And nothing unusual for my attack on that particular part of Suzuka. I tipped it into the last corner after coming out of the chicane, expecting the front tyre to grip as it normally would once it kissed the tarmac. Instead it let go so fast I lost control. The handlebars turned full lock, jamming my right hand between the bike and the ground. With the weight of the bike forcing it into the abrasive tarmac, it was as if the back of my hand had got caught in some kind of meat grinder. I left the back of my hand, including tendons, bone, muscle, and blood on the Suzuka surface that day. No glove around at the time could have protected me in such a situation. There was 160 kgs of motorcycle forcing the back of my hand into the surface as I slid down the track at 140 km/h.

Crashes happen so fast you barely have time to blink. I always jump back up immediately. Even if I had two broken feet I would still jump up just to see if I could move before I fell back down. Luckily this has never happened, and I've always hit the ground with my feet ready to get out of the way of any following traffic, even if I have limped and hobbled to the side of the track. My feet and legs were fine this time but I knew that there was something wrong with my hand. It was a bloody mess. It took some time to get my glove off as my little finger was stuck. The middle knuckle was missing, leaving my pinkie clinging on by skin alone. It was hard to peel what was left of the glove off the hand, with the knowledge that pulling too hard might totally remove my little finger. But motorcycle racers quickly learn that gear has to be removed immediately before any swelling sets in. A trick of the trade I had learnt the hard way.

The marshals called the ambulance to come and get me, but it would have to drive around most of the 6.8 kilometre circuit to reach me, and my pit was just 150 metres further down the track. I didn't want to wait for treatment, and wandered towards my pit in semi-shock. Mark Woolfrey, my mechanic, had already noticed my absence out on the circuit, and was wandering up pit lane looking for his rider. Mechanics are the first to notice you are missing. Their stopwatch alerts them that you should have come around by now, and they start checking the end of pit lane to see if you're pulling in. It's not like they're really concerned for your health, their primal fear is that you may have crashed and won't be able to remount the spare machine - that you might lose too much track time, and the race as a result. Mark looked straight past me at first. It was like he didn't recognise me. He explained later that he thought I was someone else as my leathers were no longer the white and green colour that I had been wearing. They were now blood red. A main vein had been severed and was pumping out spurts of blood with each beat of my heart. By this stage there was so much blood it had stained the front of my leathers. My boots looked like those of a freezing worker after a hard shift on the killing floor. I looked like a film extra who'd escaped the set of the *Texas Chainsaw Massacre*.

When I arrived at the medical centre I was still thinking - it's just a couple of broken bones to mend. It's just a few stitches. I'll be all right. My tolerance to pain has always been high, so I was only thinking about getting it fixed as soon as possible, and getting on with the business of winning at Suzuka. I wasn't really paying any attention to the pain. Or rather the lack of it. It's a rule of war and motorcycle racing that the worst injuries are the ones you can't feel.

The Suzuka paramedics immediately stopped the bleeding by stitching the severed vein and then I was taken directly to the hospital where the cleaning procedure began. A local anaesthetic was put into my arm and a screen put up so I couldn't see or feel a thing. I could still hear, though, and listened as the nurses scrubbed the wound out with a fingernail brush, and then a toothbrush, to remove any grit, gravel or grass. They must have done a great job, as there was never any infection. Given the extremity of the injury infection was always highly likely. Over the next couple of days I felt like a pincushion, pricked by I don't know how many injections of antibiotics to keep away any infection. The Japanese seem to have an injection for every reason.

A couple of days later I realised there was to be no quick fix with this injury, no simple realignment of bones and some stitches. The back of my hand was gone. It had become mincemeat for the Suzuka crows to feed on. I had lost three tendons completely, and the three fingers they controlled were now totally useless. My pinkie was missing a joint. Where the back of my hand used to be, there was now a very big hole. It had ground down to nothing. Luckily all the bones of my fingers were still present and accounted for, apart from the missing pinkie joint. All that was left was the palm of my right hand and those bones.

The Japanese hospital was dirty and after two days they still hadn't bathed me. It wasn't what you would imagine Japan to be like at all, particularly if your view is based on their bike racing mechanics in their immaculate white overalls. I didn't like the idea of having any operation there, so I decided to fly back to New Zealand for treatment. It was no contest really.

Mark had contacted my family in New Zealand, preparing them for my return and to get them to start looking for a surgeon. He spared them the details. At this stage, I didn't want to worry them too much. Prior to my arrival he gave them another call, warning them I could be in a wheelchair and that both my hands were damaged and out of action. During the crash my other hand was slammed down so hard onto the tarmac it had swollen to monstrous proportions and the fingertips had blood oozing out of them, trying to release the pressure. Not a pretty sight.

Mark flew back with me, as I couldn't even take myself to the toilet. He even bathed me before the flight, as the hospital staff were obviously not going to. Kawasaki had upgraded my ticket to first class so I would be more comfortable. I had one hand bandaged up like some big white fist and the other just looked like a club. I couldn't even buckle up my seat belt. Mark had a business class ticket, but there was a spare seat beside me in first. I asked the flight attendants if Mark could possibly come and sit with me, as I needed his help with absolutely everything. They refused to let him have the empty seat so I had no choice but to go back to business class and join him. This was one of many experiences with unhelpful airlines over the years, and the increasing incidents of air rage come as no surprise to me. I demanded a refund on my first class ticket - which I got. But it was no compensation. This would still be the most uncomfortable flight of my life.

My family met me in Wellington and took me straight to the public hospital there. They were shocked at my condition and concerned about what was going to happen next. The hospital staff tried to convince Megan she shouldn't look at my injuries, as they would upset her. She kept insisting on seeing my hand. I said maybe it was better if she didn't, and that the staff were right - it was horrendous to look at. "How can I understand how hurt you are if you won't let me look at your injuries?" she replied. The nurse removed the bandages, and Megan's face showed both shock and concern. There it was - my backless hand. At least the fingers were intact, and I still had my fingernails. The hand had swollen so badly that the hole was now about an inch deep and about two and a half inches in width and length.

It was great to be home but I worried about how they could fix the damage, continually going over the questions in my mind. How were tendons replaced? Would they remove the little finger? What about all the meat, muscle and general tissue that was gone? Was racing a motorcycle still possible?

The operation I needed was called an Ulnar Flap. The process involved taking a large piece of flesh, including muscle, tissue and skin from another part of my body, and using it to fill the hole in my hand. The doctors explained it was a difficult operation and there was quite a risk the injury site would not accept the foreign graft. The Ulnar Flap procedure was a relatively new development; if my accident had happened just a couple of years earlier, my right hand would have been sewn inside my stomach for blood supply while the graft was healing.

I was transferred from Wellington to Lower Hutt Hospital's burns unit, where I was introduced to Dr David Glasson, a specialist in hand and plastic surgery. I will be forever indebted to this man; he understood immediately the implications the hand injury had for my career, and tailored his treatment towards getting me back on my bike. Dr Glasson was a keen motorsports fan and car racer himself, and knew just how much my professional sport meant to me. At this stage of my career I was relatively unknown in New Zealand and was surprised at the interest he took in my case. There wasn't really that much hope, although I played down the injury when talking to the New Zealand press. My public face was full of optimism, but inside the fear of never being able to race again was overwhelming. I told reporters I'd be back on the track in a month or two, not really knowing myself when, or if, I would be.

The Ulnar Flap was going to fill the hole in the back of my hand, but without any finger tendons my right hand would still be useless. Dr Glasson decided to use the two tendons left to operate all four fingers by splitting them and sharing each between two fingers. This was an incredible surgical feat, which successfully retained the total use of my hand. The only handicap is that I cannot use my fingers individually since they share tendons. My little finger and ring finger share the former's tendon and move like Siamese twins, and the two closest to my thumb also share the index finger tendon. They operate in tandem. Injuries such as this are lessons in anatomy. I now have a greater understanding of how my body works, and marvel at the machinery of muscles, tendons, bones, and nerves.

Dr Glasson chose my right forearm as the donor site for the Ulnar Flap material. He thought that as I was already disfigured on that side, he might as well keep the left arm looking pristine. From here he removed bone, muscle, and all the meat and skin, leaving another ugly hole in my forearm. This was covered with a skin graft from my thigh. The scar that remains on my forearm alone is horrific. It looks like I've had an argument with a chainsaw. People who don't know me often see this before they notice the reconstructive scars on my hand. I've grown used to the bulging eyes and sharp intakes of breath that accompany the first sight of my right forearm. Given there is no fat layer to hide or protect the remaining muscle there, it is like a window into my body with a view of how my forearm operates. The skin covering it has not hidden the movement of tendons and muscles. It is quite strange watching your body move and work through only the thin outer layer of your skin. It's also not the method I'd recommend for lowering the body's fat levels.

The bone taken from my forearm was used to fuse a permanent joint for my little finger. The joint would never move again, and normally Dr Glasson would have set it slightly bent. But we decided to hook it into the shape of a handlebar, just in case I could race again. Besides, I didn't want to hold a glass or drink a cup of tea with my pinkie sticking straight out.

After the operation my hand looked like something out of *The Elephant Man*. The Ulnar Flap was huge and stuck out the top of my hand like some grotesque bulge. I was told the swelling would reduce and my hand would look more normal over time. The pain was more of a problem than the disfigurement. Morphine and me don't go together. It was not doing anything to help me. I couldn't get enough of it for it to be effective. The pain was so incredible I was having 'arm blocks', local anaesthetics to keep the arm dead. Every time I had an arm block it seemed to wear off a couple of hours earlier than the last, and the nurses, concerned about dependency, would leave me suffering until my next scheduled shot.

It was three or four weeks of agony before I could begin physiotherapy. By then, the Flap had successfully grafted to the hand. My forearm was also healing well. I was looking forward to getting down to the work required to get my right hand operating again.

I left hospital and returned to my father's home in Masterton where Megan was now living. I had now been given a physio schedule and met another special person who helped me get back to full fitness and racing. Gail Donaldson was more than a physiotherapist; she was like a personal trainer. I'd spend a couple of hours in the morning with Gail, and again in the afternoon after a lunch break. During that break, I would often visit Debbie and Jimmy Goodin, friends from my old racing days in New Zealand. They were good company on our trips to Wanganui and the South Island over the Christmas holidays, and became close family friends. Jimmy had been sidecar passenger for Dick Leopard and had many New Zealand titles under his belt. It was good to spend time with them, talking about racing rather than physiotherapy.

I had to get myself to the Hutt Hospital, which was over an hour away from Masterton. So the purchase of a new car was necessary. I arrived home one day with a second-hand Toyota Celica, grinning from ear to ear. Megan was impressed and my excuse was I had to have a nice car, one easy to drive over the hill as I still couldn't use my hand. My hand on the wheel also had to change gears, and I'd lock the wheel with my knees, and shift with my good left hand. It was my first really nice car.

So off I went to Lower Hutt four days a week while Dad and Megan went off to work in Masterton. Gail and I quickly discovered the tendons had healed onto the wall of my hand and could not move freely. Tendons move through a system like a tunnel and because I had been immobile for so long they had welded themselves to the side of this tunnel, restricting their movement. Gail and I were haggling for another operation called a 'carpel tunnel' to release the tendons, and this lobbying took months.

It was during physio that I discovered I had another injury from the crash. I had cracked the ball in my shoulder joint of my right arm. This had now mended, but the calcification around the crack was reducing movement and strength in my shoulder. I had several x-rays with dye injections, and the doctors worked out that if they gave me some steroid injections into the shoulder it would allow the calcification to break down and give me freedom to move my shoulder.

All the while, Kawasaki Australia were calling trying to get a definitive answer as to whether the doctors thought it was possible for me to race again. I was due to join Rob Phillis in the World Superbike Championships the following year and they needed some commitment.

I honestly didn't know what to tell them. Dr Glasson was still not making any promises I'd get complete recovery of my hand. The healing was taking time, and I really did not know if I was ever going to race again. I wanted a definitive answer as much as Kawasaki did. I was depressed during these times of doubt. I needed motivation and positive energy to work hard to even stand a chance of getting my life back. I was 24 years old and growing up fast.

I continued my physio with Gail, and had a traction system attached to my hand, which I wore at home exercising the fingers all the time. The tendons moving my fingers down were no problem but I had to keep exercising the upward movement, using the traction mechanism to automatically return them to the upright position. The pain during my physio sessions was dealt with by inhaling laughing gas. My days with Gail were now hard work as Dr Glasson had said the tendons were strong so I should push past the pain barriers to improve their movement.

Four months went by and now I had some movement in my fingers. It was enough to encourage me to try racing again, so I went and did the Australian round of the World Superbike Championship. There's nothing like chucking yourself in the deep end of the pool to see if you can swim! I didn't drown, finishing with an eighth and a seventh, but I came away disheartened. I couldn't hold the handlebars as tightly as I needed to, as the right hand simply didn't have the grip. The next weekend I competed at the New Zealand round of the World Series. In the first race the bike stopped with a broken alternator wire. In the second I made the Manfield podium by finishing third. With a stronger right hand, a WSC win in front of my home crowd could have been on the cards.

Gail and I eventually convinced Dr Glasson to perform the carpel tunnel operation. While he was freeing up my tendons he decided to do a little plastic surgery. He nipped and tucked around my little finger to separate it from the hand and the edges of the flap, reducing the bulge on top of my hand. Opening the flap, he worked on the tendons making new channels for them to move freely through. I was a new man, both practically and cosmetically.

The minute I woke up from this operation I was told I must start working the fingers straight away. It was not a great sight as the blood oozed out the wounds. The movement aggravated the blood flow, but I wasn't discouraged. I needed the movement, and nothing was going to stop me racing now. I had a drain bag attached to my hand to catch the excess fluids. This gory appendage didn't stop me getting up from my hospital bed and walking down to the local fish and chip shop for a celebratory feed.

The four months I spent recovering from the hand injury gave me time to think about my racing. I concluded that I wouldn't succeed on balls alone. Talent and aggression will only take you so far in this gladiatorial sport. I had been given a second chance and did not want it to end in a hospital bed like this again. Before the crash I would just go as fast as I could without realising how or why. This approach ended in tears many times. Now I wanted to be a more complete racer who could not only win races but championships too. I was now ready to finish for points when necessary to achieve the ultimate goal - World Champion.

To achieve this lofty goal, I decided I had to be prepared to let my ego take a knock occasionally, and accept that I wasn't the fastest rider on that particular day. But I wouldn't let these setbacks knock back my confidence, or shake the belief I had in my ability on any race day. I decided to swot up on my technical skills, to have a better understanding of what the bike needed changing to tailor it to each track. I also wanted to be the fittest rider in the paddock. The one who could go hardest on the last lap of any race, no matter how long, and whatever weather conditions were prevalent at the time. The year 1990 was a turning point for me, for a more mature attitude emerged from all those hours of reflection on the hospital bed.

That summer, while still working on getting my hand back into shape, I bought a speedboat, as extra therapy. My mates and I would go down to the Diversion, a river near Masterton, and we spent the summer learning to water ski. This helped rebuild the strength in my hand. Strenuous recreation is great motivation for keeping fit, and the skiing was great for building my upper body and hand strength. I called the bright orange boat *Far Canal*.

The second operation on the carpel tunnels made all the difference. This was a huge milestone for me. My hand worked; a little oddly, and probably not the best to look at, but I was going back to racing at peak ability. Getting change out of my pocket is still difficult as my permanently bent pinkie causes some problems off the bike. On the bike it's perfect. A scientifically tailored hand for killing speed, two fingers operating in tandem on the brake lever, finely-tuned in sensitivity. Then two fingers operating in tandem while gripping the handlebar. I used to be a 'four-finger' man on the brake lever. From that day on I used two, while the pinkie and its mate hooked the bar. I guess you could say it worked for me.

My return to racing was a huge relief. The days of depression and doubt were over. I was back, and I was going to prove myself once and for all, with a new attitude to apply. I knocked off the 1991 Australian Superbike Championship in style. Then the Pan-Pacific championship, with four wins from four starts. The Malaysian series was mine for the taking. It was wham, bam, thank you ma'am. We moved to Surfers' Paradise, which was where we had been heading before the crash in Japan, and restarted our lives. It was a perfect year. The wins against guys like Campbell, Goddard, Crafar and Scott Doohan seemed to come easy, and they reinforced my belief in myself with or without the handicap of my hand. Racing had resumed, but so had the politics of it all. Not only had I recovered my speed, I had lifted my technical game, but I had yet to learn how to walk the walk through professional racing's political world.

When Ago lost the factory Yamahas in '89 I lost my first opportunity of a 500 ride. Now the dream of racing in 500GP came around to tempt me again in the negotiating season towards the end of 1991. My comeback had been so spectacular, more than superbike teams started putting offers my way as my Kawasaki contract started to run out.

Peter Doyle, the team manager of the Kawasaki World Superbike team, was pushing me to renew a contract for 1992. This was a great opportunity to follow Rob Phillis into the World Superbike Championship. Rob had left Australia in 1990 to race in the world championship and we were great friends. Joining him and his family in Europe was a great chance for me. If I took it, I would work with people I knew and a team I liked.

But a 500 ride was also a possibility, again as a teammate to Kevin Schwantz. Motor-journalist Peter Clifford, who had initiated the 1989

Agostini talks, was still putting the word around the Grand Prix paddock about me. He talked to Garry Taylor, manager of the Lucky Strike Suzuki team, who expressed an interest in signing me. I was immediately keen. The team was strong and it was the 500s after all - the Formula One of motorcycle racing. It was a serious offer and we got down to talking dollars and cents. All the while I had Peter Doyle on my back pushing me to sign for the World Superbike Championship with Kawasaki. He was telling me to "forget all that GP shit" and sign with them. I was trying to buy some time, so I kept putting Peter off, waiting on Garry Taylor to finalise the deal with Suzuki. It got to the point where I asked Peter for two more weeks to finalise my decision, but he said: "If you don't sign today, it is all over."

I immediately contacted Garry for a letter of intent or something solid from him and his team to show a commitment to me for the next season. Nothing came. It turned out Garry had been stringing me along, and I had now put myself in a bad position with Kawasaki. Garry signed Didier de Radigues as his second rider. This was not a decision based on performance as Didier was on the verge of retirement. Rumour had it that he was bringing personal sponsorship to the team and that fitted the way Garry Taylor operated. I was really disappointed Garry had led me on, and then dumped me at the 11th hour for somebody with more money. It was clear he regarded the extra dollars as more important than my talent. Garry puffed out his budget with the extra sponsorship, and obviously thought he had all the riding talent he needed in Schwantz. He took a short-term gain in favour of long-term success. It probably never occurred to him Kevin might crash himself out of the 500 Championship.

Back to Kawasaki I went, to sign the World Superbike Championship deal they had offered me. But the to-and-fro with Suzuki had put me in a weaker negotiating position. The deal was slashed from a full championship contract to a participation agreement for 11 out of the 13 races. The reason given was that I had to be in Japan for some testing on those weekends. This was just a show of power. I was convinced it was bullshit as I signed the contract, and my suspicions were right. There was no reason I shouldn't have raced those two Italian rounds of the 1992 World Superbike Championship. My services weren't required in Japan. My bikes were in Europe; in fact the whole team was there. I just wasn't allowed to race. This was punishment for not agreeing to Peter's terms when it suited him. The other rod Team Green applied to my back for playing hard-to-get was an $A20,000 cut in salary.

So Garry Taylor got his meal ticket at my expense, and his one truly talented rider was Kevin Schwantz. I followed the progress of the Suzuki team over the years and nothing changed. Throughout the early 1990s, Garry had Kevin to win, and someone to bring in the dollars. Every teammate to Suzuki's number one rider from that day on was there for some political reason or the money they bought to the team. Garry didn't seem to worry about where his 'cash cows' ran in the field. They were the easiest factory riders on the 500 grid to beat. At least he gave the privateers someone to aim for and beat.

Despite the cut in races and salary, I wasn't bitter. The 1992 Kawasaki deal was the big break I was looking for. It was a two-year contract with all the 1993 WSC races included. So I could go to Europe with the attitude of learning the circuits in 1992 for my full onslaught the following year. It put me on schedule with a chance to win a world title by the time I was 27. I was off to race in Europe with a factory bike under me. Off to become a real World Championship contender for the first time. I was 26, with plenty of good races left in me. That fateful Thursday afternoon at Suzuka hadn't snuffed out my dreams. What could have so easily been the end, turned out to be the beginning. Against all odds, a Kiwi had finally gained full factory support on the World Superbike stage.

six

Taking on The World

Pulling on my leathers as a full factory rider contending the world Superbike championship for the first time was a proud moment, but I would have felt even prouder had there been the logo of a New Zealand company stitched onto them. I still don't know why New Zealand companies see niche sports such as rugby as their best opportunities for global publicity. Motorcycle racing has a huge global TV audience, and attracts some of the biggest crowds in sport. A Spanish Grand Prix or a Suzuka 8-Hour can pull in up to 180,000 spectators at the track, and the TV ratings are right up there with Formula One car racing. F1 boss Bernie Ecclestone was quick to see the spectacle in motorcycle racing, and quickly got involved with the Grand Prix side. He could see a growing TV audience, and massive exposure for sponsors. Yet New Zealand corporations seeking a higher global profile seem blind to the opportunities that motorsport presents. Perhaps motorsport is considered incompatible with the "clean, green" image New Zealand likes to present.

Another factor is the low profile of bike racing in the New Zealand media. I would soon become better known in Europe than in New Zealand. Even today, I can walk down a Wellington street in relative anonymity. It's hard for New Zealand's corporate world to relate to sports that don't receive coverage back home. My World Superbike wins were 20-second sound-bytes on New Zealand TV. Those that wanted to see me race back there had to subscribe to pay TV.

Halfway through 1991 I got a new Kawasaki superbike to ride, and it was a flyer. Rob had been racing it in the World Series all year, and sometimes bought it back to Australia for a round of the national Superbike championship. My last race on the old bike was in Tasmania, and I really wanted to prove that I was as fast on the old bike as Rob was on the new. He just beat me in the first round, which really fired me up. I was leading the second race when I ran off while trying to make a gap on the field. He came past, and probably wondered what the hell I was up to. As I got back on the track I was livid. I rejoined the race in 12th, put my head down and rode the wheels off the old machine. I passed all the Aussie championship contenders, blew right by Campbell, Scott Doohan and co., to finish second behind Rob.

On the new bike I was virtually unbeatable when it came to either the Australian or Pan-Pacific Superbike championships. The Pan-Pacific rounds were more international including the Aussies, the local Japanese talent and Kiwi riders, yet that championship was a clean sweep for me. Four wins from four starts. One of the few times I got beaten in regional racing during that year was in the Aussie championship round at Lakeside in Queensland. I took all the skin off the knuckles of my good hand in a practice crash on Saturday afternoon, and arrived at the track with my arm in a sling on raceday. Once again I was giving my glove supplier - Kushitani - plenty of test data as I wouldn't let go of the bars this time either.

A cold rear tyre had stepped out on me while exiting Hungry corner - a gnarly uphill left-hander. I landed heavily on my left hand, and it almost became a mirror of the right. The back of the pinkie was ground away, exposing the finger tendon and the hand was once again swollen to look like a club. The doctor told me I shouldn't race the next day. But there was a championship to win, and I knew that if I could keep it upright, I'd be in the points. Scott Doohan, on the Peter Jackson Yamaha, won both races on his home track, while I followed him home in second. But I should have won, the injury and Doohan's home track advantage took away my edge. When I set a new lap record chasing Doohan home in the second race, I kicked myself for making the mistake in practice. The ego-buzz of having to be fastest on Saturday had cost me dearly. It was one of the few times I lapsed back into my old race instincts, and it was the only opportunity I gave my Australian Championship rivals of beating me. Most of the other rounds I dominated despite big bucks efforts from Honda, Yamaha, and Suzuki. No one had put such a stamp on the Australian championship before. Out of the 12 championship races, I scored seven wins, four seconds, and one third.

Perhaps I should have had the attitude that Lakeside was also my home track at the time, for Megan and I were looking after Mick Doohan's mother's house on the Gold Coast nearby. Colleen Doohan and husband Ken were in Europe driving Mick's motorhome around the Grand Prix circuit. I had first met Mick in the Yamaha 250 production days, and as our career paths kept crossing, we became friends, as did Scott and Jady Doohan, and their two daughters.

Surfers Paradise is the Monaco of Australia. The climate matches the luxurious lifestyle, and provided you can put up with the Huntsman spiders, which are as big as your hand, and iguana-sized lizards crawling around your back yard, it's as good a place as any to live. We were now settled into a large family home with a pool, and we were very happy. Megan did not work as I was earning enough money now to support us both so she began coming to the races frequently. We became close friends with Darryl Beattie as he was now competing in the F1 championship for Honda in Japan. He would fly to and from every race meeting, and in between would scare us senseless in the Surfers Paradise broadwater and canals in his new ski boat. One day we left Megan on the shore as we did a "fly by," and she reckons she saw both sides of the hull as the boat tip-toed through the water, and nearly turned over backwards. A favourite spot to go water skiing was off Barry Sheene's private little beach. But we stopped going there as soon as we heard that a triathlete had been bitten by a shark in these canals.

In the three rounds of the World Superbike championship I got to do at the end of 1991, I got on the podium twice in six races. First up was the Japanese round at Sugo, where I finished second overall after scoring a third in the first race, and a fourth in the second.

On the last lap of the second race I was dicing with Kevin Magee for third position. On the run out of the last chicane I had much better drive than Kevin and was accelerating past him up the hill. He ran me right out to the white line as I was passing around the outside. As I went by he took his left hand off the handlebar, grabbed me on the right knee and using me as leverage. At the time it was a bit of a laugh as we were looking over at each other, but when I realised he had beaten me by a tyre width, the smile quickly faded. I don't think Kevin realised what the consequences would be at the time. It was really just a practical joke - one that would help him onto the podium. Kevin and I still laugh about that manoeuvre today. Doug Polen won both legs on his factory Ducati, on his way to the title. Apart from his teammate Raymond Roche, Rob Phillis was Polen's main opponent that year, but was finding it tough racing a heavier 750cc four against 1000cc twins allowed a 25 kg weight break. Rob finished second in the first leg, but crashed out of the second. Meanwhile someone named Carl Fogarty finished the second race in eighth place on the Honda Britain RC30. Carl never really featured or shone during 1991.

Rob and I qualified on the front row in Malaysia, but it was another Ducati double, this time with Roche taking the top place on the podium in each race. Rob's woes continued when he finished fifth in the first race, and had a DNF in the second after a fork seal blew and covered his brakes with fork oil. I finished with a seventh and a fourth, crossing the line in the second race close behind a freight train of Ducati riders headed for the podium - Roche, Mertens, and Polen.

At the Aussie round of the WSC at Phillip Island, I came away with a Superbike lap record, but still no first win. Perhaps I should have won there, but as usual, it was anyone's race. Phillip Island is one of the best circuits in the world when it comes to encouraging close races. In the first race, I set a new lap record as three of us went for the race win. As we crossed the line the officials awarded the race to Kevin Magee, on a Yamaha, Doug Polen and then myself. I'm still not convinced that the officials got it right as it was so tight at the front. Their call really made Doug jump up and down at the time. In the second race, I got a good start, but my bike started to misfire and on lap eight I was taken out by Stephane Mertens at MG corner. Phillip Island's amazing; the place is inspiring. There's a mixture of everything - a corner for every gear, and a mixture of long and short straights in between. But you need to dig deep for a hot lap. The Japanese riders I met in my Kawasaki and Honda days hated testing there. They were hopeless when faced with such a naturally dramatic racetrack that demands a complete rider. You've got to show all of your skills at the Island.

Especially fast corner skills. Racing all comes down to finding another 100th of a second on the other guy. At a fast track like PI, Hockenheim, or Monza - with its awesome fourth gear corners - if you can go around that sweeper 1 km/h faster than the rest it makes a big difference to the lap time. But it's hard finding that extra speed without also finding the edge, and the consequences of crashing at 250 km/h are huge. All those hours on the hospital bed in '90 got me thinking about all the times I went over the edge. I knew better where the limit was, and how to find it.

When I raced WSC at the Island in '91, the lap record proved I'd dialled in my bike best to the circuit. So I wasn't happy when the Kawasaki started spluttering and misfiring eight laps into the second race. Especially after just missing out on the first race. The DNF made me all the more determined to reach the top of the WSC podium in 1992.

I arrived in Europe for the first round of the 1992 World Superbike Championship at Albacete, a new track in eastern Spain. It was a paddock of rookies coming to grips with a new track. No one had ridden it before. There were mutterings of discontent all over the pits about the stop/start nature of the new track's layout. But I sure liked it. In years to come Albacete would be the scene of many Ducati victories, as their extra grunt and traction off the corners would make them hard to beat there. Not this day though. For the first race of the 1992 season belonged to Kawasaki. And me.

But it was an opportunist win, one won through my skill at getting the bike quickly dialled in, and my ability to instantly find the limit in wet conditions. The four cylinder bikes have traction problems at Albacete. They spin up the rear wheel exiting the tight corners, where the twins just hook up and drive. The elation of my first WSC win was short-lived. By the second race, the track was drying and Raymond Roche found his confidence had returned on the factory Ducati, and as much as Kawasaki's stable of riders - me, Rob, Terry Rymer, and Scott Russell - tried, we could no longer stem the red bike tide. I crashed, when hitting a wet patch with the front tyre and was bought back to earth rather quickly. It was a huge crash, but I walked away. Rob finished second, and Roche won, with Ducati-mounted Daniel Armatrain taking the last place on the podium. My first European round of the World Championship had produced the highest of highs, and the lowest of lows. It was a lesson, and I got to know that the closer you get to winning the title, then the higher those peaks become. Unfortunately, it's also true that the depths become deeper as well.

It's the nature of the World Superbike beast that riders winning the first race of the two-race format don't really get to celebrate their win. For there's always the thoughts of the second race hanging over their heads, and getting up on the podium is no opportunity to relax. So celebrations at Albacete were subdued. The team knew the Ducatis would come back stronger in the second race. Meanwhile if team manager Peter Doyle regretted his cutting short of my championship effort that year after that first race win, he didn't show it. I had come to Europe for the first time and had won my very first race, and was convinced that, with the right package, I could be world champion.

In the 1992 Kawasaki crew I had the right team, but not the right bike. Although the Kawasaki ZXR750 superbikes were the fastest of the 750cc fours at the time, they couldn't quite cut it in a championship where the rules were so heavily stacked in the favour of the 1000cc V-twins. Rob Phillis gave his all to Kawasaki during the early 1990s but never won the championship. Scott Russell, the hard-charging American from Georgia, would go on to win the 1993 World Superbike Championship for Kawasaki, but it's probably fair to say that Ducati lost that year, rather than Kawasaki won. Meanwhile it's easy to speculate at what my team might have achieved in 1992 had we been racing V-twins.

For I had some of the best people in bike racing around me. Team manager Peter Doyle was the best I met at extracting the maximum performance from his team, and he was very much in control. An Australian hard man, he'd quickly cut through the bullshit to sort out any problem or issue. Peter has always looked after number one and wasn't out to make friends. He built a successful life in the process.

He ran a very tight ship with limited budgets but got great results for the money. He had travelled to Europe at the age of 15 with his father Neville so he had a wealth of knowledge about the logistics of bike racing there. He worked hard and thought constantly about racing, but he also knew how to party hard too. I think Peter was a wannabe racer. He made a better team manager than a rider judging by the huge crashes he told me about in his early days. Today he is successfully looking after Matt Mladin in America.

I knew little about fellow Kiwi Adrian Gorst until he was signed to be my chief mechanic for the 1992 Moving Kawasaki team. He was to be my chief mechanic until the end of 1997. Adrian seemed to have the basic kiwi skill - ingenuity - the classic ability to make anything out of number eight fencing wire. A very hard worker, he would leave no stone unturned, and his bike preparation bordered on the fastidious. We had a good working relationship, one that kept us at the top of our game for six years. When he later followed me to Castrol Honda, Adrian settled in Louth, England, where the team is based, with his wife Alison and had their two children. Their door was always open to me. This was something I really appreciated, as there were a few large nights out in Louth where I would stagger back to their house. In the early days with Castrol Honda, Adrian and I formed the technical foundations of the team. I'll never forget the day we went to see the new Castrol Honda transporter for the new season. Everybody was in awe over this shiny new semi-trailer, as it was a huge boost in team image. It had bunks and TVs in every room, but Adrian was less than impressed: "So where do we put the fucking bikes?" was his first question. They had loaded the transporter up with so many luxuries; it would only fit three of the team's four bikes in the space left. The comment was classic Adrian. His thoughts were always on racing and his rider 24 hours a day.

Fast-talking Texan Doug Polen had dominated the 1991 World Superbike Championship, winning 17 of the 24 races. In 1992 he wouldn't have it so easy, the Kawasaki was a more sorted machine - there was a bit more power, a more rigid frame, and more traction to control it with. Rob held the points lead through the early part of the season. Polen would eventually overtake him, and as soon as Rob lost the points lead, his usual run of late season bad luck returned. But the real reason Polen wasn't the force he was in 1991, was the emergence of other riders on the red bikes. Ducati had produced a special run of 30 888 Corsas for the 1992 season, and these were eagerly snapped up by anyone keen to make a name for themselves in World Superbike. There was the wild Giancarlo Falappa, who took his 888 Ducati by the scruff of the neck, and chucked it around like it was the motocross bike he learned to race on, earning "The Hardman" tag from the press. He won an awesome double in Austria, tearing the other Ducati riders apart. There was Belgian veteran Stephane Mertens, and Spanish young blood Daniel Armatrain also flying the Ducati flag high. Then there was Carl Fogarty, who found a private Ducati 888 Corsa a lot more competitive than the Honda RC30 V4 he had raced the year before. Carl plucked the eyes out of the championship in '92, mainly taking on the tracks he knew best - Donington, Assen, Zeltweg etc. He finished ninth in the championship despite skipping five rounds.

Fogarty was the other debutante winner of the class of 1992. He won the second race at Donington Park in the UK, followed home by Roche and Russell. It was a fine illustration of just how good the 888 Corsa was. The only difference between the privateer Ducati 888 Corsas and the factory bikes of Roche and Polen was that they weighed five kgs more. At 147 kgs, they were still 18 kgs lighter than the 165 kg minimum weight limit of the 750cc fours. Fogarty went from zero to hero that day. At the previous round at Albacete, he'd finished 10th and 12th in the two races.

There was no better illustration of Ducati's dominance in 1992 than qualifying for the Spanish round at Jarama circuit. Polen got pole, Mertens was second fastest, then Fogarty, Armatrain, and Falappa. A red bike clean sweep of the front row of the grid, and Fogarty's and Armatrain's bikes were off-the-shelf privateer bikes, things anyone could buy straight off the showroom floor. It was my first time at Jarama, and I qualified 11th while Rob earned seventh spot on the grid. On the Kawasakis the power delivery was quite peaky, and Jarama's up and down corners and bumps didn't suit me on the ZXR. I had to be smooth getting on the power, as hitting the bumps when the top end power came in would send the bike tank-slapping down the next stretch. Meanwhile the smooth mid range performance of the twins allowed them to get on the gas early, and grunt away into the distance.

By the end of the championship, Ducati riders had won 20 of the 26 races. Yamaha won three with Fabrizio Pirovano's double in the wet at Monza, and Kevin Magee's win-by-photo-finish at Phillip Island. Kawasaki scored three wins - my Albacete victory, and two wins for Rob. This was an early illustration of the way the rules favoured the larger twins. Of the 26 races, six were shared by the Japanese 750 fours - an average of 1.5 per each manufacturer taking part. We'd given our all, and Rob finished third in the championship, while I finished sixth. Yet we felt like we deserved more success, especially in light of the living conditions we endured throughout the season.

As an Australian and a New Zealander contesting a championship primarily centred in Europe, we couldn't go home after each race. The Europeans could go home on Sunday nights, see the family, and live in a style approaching normalcy. Rob and I would return to our team's headquarters in Freidrichsdorf, Germany. There he would repark his caravan and would stay with Carol and the kids at the back of the workshop. I would return with Megan to the pokey little bed and breakfast the team was staying in. In those days Kawasaki Germany's workshop backed onto a forest and it was quite a nice setting where Rob and Carol had set up their home. It wasn't luxurious by any means, but they had a place to call their own. And a car.

Megan and I started hitching lifts with Adrian and the mechanics to Kawasaki each day, anything to escape the B&B, which was stuck out in the middle of nowhere. We were in Euro-shock, with little spare money to spend, and no means of getting around. We'd wait for the mechanics to finish their day's work, follow them to the pub where they would play darts and drink copious amounts of German beer. Anything not to return to that lonely B&B. We'd be stuck there in that B&B limbo for up to two weeks at a time. Then we'd suddenly head to a hotel somewhere near the next race. Then back to Germany again. It was like we never grounded. Homeless.

Competitors from outside the continent do it tough in Europe. I've seen many an American racer crack under Europe's weight, and they don't have a 36-hour flight to get home. There's the language barriers. There really wasn't much point Megan and me learning the various languages. By the time we learned how to say the basics in Spanish, we'd be in Czechoslovakia, and learning all over again. English and Italian were the two main languages of the Superbike paddock, but I've always ridden for Japanese brands, so there was the language of my bike manufacturer to consider as well. There's the food. We never got used to the sausages, cheese and rolls that our German hosts preferred for breakfast. We would take our box of cereal up to breakfast, and be laughed at, as that was considered food for kinder (children). The mechanics would also bowl in with their jar of vegemite for their toast. Then there's the hotels and the living out of suitcases. I have yet to unpack my faithful Country Road toilet bag. It has been lived out of for over 10 years, globe-trotting the world with its owner. Megan at least tries to unpack her overstuffed makeup bag, placing its contents into the hotels drawers on arrival. It helps her feel kind of normal. I don't bother.

Fortunately the people at Kawasaki were really nice, and every Friday night they would put on a BBQ for the riders, mechanics, and families that treated their head office like a home away from home. We'd enjoy those Friday nights, then watch as the Kawasaki staff drifted off to their homes with envy.

I'm sure Megan didn't enjoy hanging out at the workshop. We were lucky to have the Phillis family there. In New Zealand, the Maori people call extended families whanau. We became part of the Phillis whanau, a surrogate Aunt and Uncle to Rob and Carol's kids. Megan and Carol would drink endless cups of tea and dunk biscuits all day long to pass the hours, frustrated that there were no other options. We couldn't afford to rent a car to go sightseeing. We were in survival mode. I told Megan that the following year we'd have a motorhome, and a life of our own. I was prepared to do anything to race at the highest level, stay anywhere between races if that's what it took. But it's different when there's another person to consider as well, and although Megan didn't complain much, I yearned to be able to provide her with a better life.

Like a lot of Kiwi and Aussie kids we kept ourselves amused by our surroundings. Rob and I were big kids at heart with a lot of time to spare. So we would try and amuse our families by our antics. First we tried flat-tracking minibikes on the cobblestones behind the head office workshops. Then the mechanics joined in, and we soon had a section through the forest that we used to time. The mechanics set the "no protection" rule as they thought that if we were protected they wouldn't stand a chance. Everyone raced in shorts and jandals (thongs) - no helmets, gloves, boots, or armour. They really should have changed the rules after a few beers. There were some awful alcohol-fuelled crashes, but no one felt any pain at the time. Upon Scott Russell's introduction to life at Friedericksdorf the following year he turned up to race the minibike in full kit, and was laughed back to his motorhome. "Don't be a girl!" shouted all the Aussie mechanics.

Over winter Rob made a spa pool out of motorcycle crates, and he would bathe in it even when it was snowing. Rob can make anything out of nothing and many a BBQ was had with Rob's innovation.

Sometimes I would wonder about where the makeshift BBQ grille had come from. I would always insist on stoking up the fire to get maximum sterilisation. John Kocinski would have had 40 fits.

The best times were packing up, and driving to a race. Megan and I would join Peter and his girlfriend Diana, and a couple of mechanics, in a Transit van and drive 16 hours or so to a race. Usually Rob would head off the day before with caravan and family in tow. That might not sound like fun, but we would feel happier as we were doing what we came to Europe to do. We would now be a key component in the team, rather than hangers-on. There was a lot of camaraderie and ANZAC spirit in that Aussie-Kiwi Kawasaki camp. Which made it even more unsettling when we were told that the World Superbike effort would be run by Rob Muzzy, the American exhaust pipe manufacturer, for the following season.

It wasn't so much a big change as a strange change. We had been running on a tight budget. We used team vans to get to races where other teams hired their riders rental cars. Rob and Carol would tow the caravan to each race, and it was a factory team run on a shoestring. Now Rob Muzzy would get a fat pay cheque to be the chief, and he quickly hired Peter Doyle to do the team management work for him. So I had the same people around me, except for the Phillis family. With the change, Rob got kicked out, replaced by Scott Russell, the 1992 AMA Superbike champion. There was no way Rob wanted to finish that year. He was around 34 at the time, and riding as hard as ever. His 1992 victory at Jarama had been won by sheer determination and aggression. The qualifying sessions had clearly shown he was on the wrong bike to win there. But he had reached an age the Japanese manufacturers seem to consider a rider's use-by date. After three years of hard slog for Kawasaki in Europe, he and his family were going home.

What made the sacking a bitter pill for Rob to swallow was that he could see 1993 shaping up as Kawasaki's best chance ever to win the World Superbike title. Ducati had confirmed that they would race the same 888 as 1992, as they were putting all their development into the new 916. Not only would the red bike be an old one, they were going to place it in young, inexperienced hands. The two Ducati riders that beat Rob in 1992 would not be on the 1993 WSC starting grid. Double world champ Doug Polen was to race in the AMA, and French veteran Raymond Roche had hung up his helmet to become a Ducati factory team manager with Fogarty and Falappa as his riders. But there would be two Ducati factory teams that year, and Kawasaki would be in a position of being able to divide and conquer. The rival squad was run by Davide Tardozzi, with Stephane Mertens and Spanish 500 star Juan Garriga in the saddles. Then there was the wild card of "The Red Brigade" - privateer Andreas Meklau, whose clever engine tuner, Edgar Schnyder, was the first Ducati engine man to take advantage of the added cubic capacity the World Superbike rules permitted to V-twins. Schnyder took the 888 engine out to 926cc, and Meklau would sweep the field at his home round in Zeltweg, Austria.

Although I thought Rob's sacking was unfair, I quickly became friends with Scott. He had the biggest heart, and so much natural talent on a motorcycle it bordered on the unnatural. He was high on life, always in fast forward mode and totally wacky by my typically reserved Kiwi standards. Scott was from Georgia with a real southern twang and a big white smile. He was also really lost in Europe. He would sleep all day just to pass the time and hang out for the return back to the U.S. It took him some time to realise that the American dollar wasn't welcome everywhere, and that he had to plan forward and exchange his money before any journeys. The U.S. dollar ruled - didn't it?

Scott travelled with his opposite personality-wise - his cousin Chris. Chris would make order of Scott's chaotic life, and was totally laid-back and non-plussed compared to the passionate, reactive Scott. Chris also became a life long friend, and two more different people you could never meet. Before the start of the season I flew out to Scott's and we both purchased an articulated motorhome, commonly called a fifth wheel, to travel around Europe in. It was a huge deal for me as I spent every last cent on it, including having to get advanced payments from Muzzy, but it meant that Megan and I would at last have a base. It was an amazing truck - a big GMC dually (single axle dual wheel pickup truck) which you hooked up to the huge caravan. The fifth wheel trailer had a pull out side which you extended when you parked up. We had more room than we could have dreamed of. More than that pokey B&B, and a home for my Country Road toilet bag. The down side was that it was not the safest of vehicles to tackle the autobahns with in bad conditions. After some serious out braking manoeuvres up the emergency lanes and near death experiences, Megan and I decided to pull over and sleep through the rough weather and make up time somewhere else along the way. The truck was the best part of the bargain. We could park the trailer and jump in the truck to escape at a moment's notice, and for the first time we visited villages all over Europe. It gave us independence from the team and from everyone. It was the hugest vehicle and on American plates, so we just parked anywhere, and risked getting a ticket. It was quite an attraction, especially in Spain, where many curious young guys would leave the side windows streaked with their hair gel. Megan always got a kick out seeing their jaws drop as she climbed in the massive GMC and drove off.

Maybe because it was the first European country I raced in, and where I had won my very first WSC race, Spain holds a special place in our hearts. More though that we love the approach to and quality of life that Spain offers. The people are friendly, the weather warm and the cost of living not as expensive as other parts of Europe. We made two great friends there, Pere and Eva, who have welcomed us to their home and Barcelona, giving us great sightseeing tours and superb seafood that Spain is famous for.

While Ducati scattered their seeds to the wind, Kawasaki was in transition. Muzzy tried to make all the parts for the bikes in his backyard in Bend, Oregon. Things that we usually got from the Kawasaki factory, like footrests, handlebars, and wheel spacers etc; Muzzy would get his own company to make. I couldn't believe these guys had won the AMA championship, because of the sub-standard gear. Scott was fast because he was Scott, and used to racing with that stuff. It would take most of the season until I was happy with the bike. Muzzy was an exhaust manufacturer, and he always tuned for top-end power. I tried to get him to realise that this approach didn't suit European tracks and the World Series. The bikes were like light switches in their power delivery. The power was all or nothing. I kept asking for more mid-range as you need torque to get off the corners. And we were racing not only the reddest bikes in the world, but the ones with the most torque. I remember watching from second place as Meklau's big-bore Duke pulled bike lengths out of me each corner exit in the first of the Austrian races, and thinking "I wish I had that grunt". You can only make up so much ground on the brakes.

Muzzy had a scatter-gun approach to bike preparation. He would only fork out the money for two sets of carbon composite disc brakes for Scott and me. Our spare bikes had steel discs up front, so they were totally useless. We only used them for wet races, and parts the rest of the time. He was so focused on saving money; our bikes were badly put together. My heart dropped to the floor at our first test at Daytona as a team. There were all these American aftermarket products all over the bikes - Fox rear shocks, Performance Machine brakes and wheels - and none of it worked as well as the stuff on the factory Kawasaki that I had the year before. I began to wonder if Muzzy had really tested this stuff, or if he had put it on the bike because of some contra deal he had with those manufacturers. At Daytona I asked Scott if he could hold the throttle wide open on the banking leading to the fast chicane. He looked at me like I'd been smoking weed. "Of course, I'm flat out through there," he replied. "Well there's no way I can, the handlebars won't stay in my hands. The head-shake is so bad, that if I try to go wide open it's going to flick me over the concrete wall."

With the knowledge that Scott wasn't having the same problem, I got Adrian to pull the front end of the bike apart, and make sure everything was right. He found the front wheel spacers had been machined to the wrong dimensions, so when tightening up the axle the wheel spacers weren't being pinched up tightly, and the wheel was wobbling all over the place.

Then there were the American bits. Performance Machine specialised in making stuff for Harleys - a soft target when it comes to making improvements. There was no way their stuff was going to stand up in the World Superbike arena, and I proved it by buckling several sets of wheels at that Daytona test. Fox were looking at breaking out into the roadbike area, and were still primarily a maker of dirtbike shocks at the time. I was used to having a factory bike arrive from Kawasaki Heavy Industries, fully sorted by the KHI test riders. Not these mongrels. They had started life as ordinary 750cc roadbikes, and it took a lot of time and effort to turn them into world-beaters.

Perhaps the biggest machine change I had to adjust to was the Dunlop tyres. I rode on Michelins prior to the year with Muzzy, and there was a huge difference in grip, and the way the tyres from the two brands would let go. The Michelins hung on longer, which suited my attack of fast corners but would let go violently and would not move forward while spinning. The Dunlops let go earlier, but in a more progressive way enabling you to oversteer while still moving forward. With the peaky power delivery of Muzzy's engines, and the lessened traction in the rear tyres, the Kawasaki would light up the rear wheel like never before. So I had to adjust my riding style to the new tyre characteristics, and it took some time to sort out. After I got used to the Dunlops I started to enjoy sliding around. Scott meanwhile charged from the beginning of the championship, as he was used to the Dunlops, used to Muzzy's obsession with peak power.

The 1993 WSC is remembered for the huge battle between Scott and Carl for the title, but it was Falappa who held the early points lead, with Russell in second. By mid-season Fogarty was on the comeback trail after crashing out at Brands Hatch. He scored doubles in Sweden where on our Muzzy bikes we were using titanium valves for the first time. The valves were not of the highest quality, and we would lose valve clearance over a 20 lap stint consequently losing a lot of engine performance. Our results suffered, Fogarty taking the double at Malaysia after his Italian teammate also crashed. Carl now emerged as Ducati's best hope for the title. When the British rider won the first race at Sugo in front of the KHI brass, it jolted the Japanese factory into action. I had finished sixth and Scott eighth, and they presented Scott with a new engine for the second race. I got nothing, but I knew the KHI mechanics pretty well by now. I went over to the truck that the new engine had miraculously appeared from, and one of the guys handed me an exhaust system in secret, and said "Here, put that on your bike". It made a huge difference, like night and day. There wasn't as much peak power, but it made the bike more rideable, with more torque through the mid-range. While Scott used the new motor to win the second race, the new exhaust lifted me to fourth. I've still got that exhaust today. I like to tell people that it fell off the back of a truck. At the end of the year, I got the mechanics to unbolt it from the bike, as it was mine - a gift from friends in Kawasaki's engine development division. I thought "Muzzy's not having that, not after everything he's put me through."

With the new exhaust, I almost had a Kawasaki superbike as good as the bike I rode in 1992. The next round was Monza, and I shocked the team by winning the first race, then finishing second to Falappa in the second. I was keen to win again at the penultimate round at Donington. The first Donington race was stopped after a few laps. At the restart Carl and Scott had new rear tyres, I didn't. It was a decision inflicted on me by the team, as I was not challenging for the championship. Also Muzzy and I had already discussed before the start of race day that if I was able to win either race and had to let Scott by that he would pay me first place bonuses. I raced the whole race with them, finishing third on a second hand tyre. So I knew upon starting the next race I would be able to win. Scott was now just nine points in front of Carl going into race two. As the race unfolded, Carl cracked under pressure again, crashing out of the race in the Craner curves. So I thought there'd be no need for team orders now, as Scott would score plenty of points over Carl. We were going hammer and tongs, racing hard, and coming together a few times, green bike versus green bike. Then Scott succumbed to the pressure and ran off the track coming onto the back straight. So I now had a good five-second lead to play with. But going past the pits the next lap around, the only thing on my board was the message "P2." I was stunned Muzzy still wanted me to throw the race Scott's way even with Carl scoring no points. So for the last three laps I was pulling monster wheelies everywhere just to prove a point. I mucked around so much that on the last lap Jamie Whitham almost passed me for second place. I think Scott didn't want to win that way either as he slowed down to crawling speed coming out of the last corner to wait for me. Muzzy paid me first place bonuses for both races that day, but I would rather have had the wins as well.

The gesture, along with my late season charge, didn't go un-noticed. After finishing third in the championship, I was now the hot property on the World Superbike scene. The two that finished in front of me - Carl and Scott - were onto good things at Ducati and Kawasaki. So I was on top of everybody's shopping list at the end of the season. I was talking with Raymond Roche about signing for Ducati, when the phone rang. It was Honda on the other end of the line.

seven

The Great White Hope

There's little doubt in my mind that Scott Russell became the 1993 World Superbike champ because he was in a Peter Doyle-led team. Scott was a typical American - brash, out there, and fast. All he wanted to do was be the fastest at each track. During qualifying, Scott would concentrate on getting pole. He'd be riding on ultra-soft 'qualifier' tyres and he'd set his bike up on them. They'd only last five laps or so, and weren't suitable for a race.

Meanwhile I'd be dialling my bike into the race tyres, setting everything up for the main event. Scott would go through three times as many tyres setting fast times, while Peter had me out doing 20 laps on race tyres so we could see how well they'd last the distance. Come race day, Scott would ask what tyres I had run that would last the race. He would throw them on, full of the confidence he gained carving fast laps on qualifiers. Without Peter forcing me to do Kawasaki's homework, I don't think Scott would have won the title.

As this was my first year racing with Dunlop tyres I hadn't yet learnt how to get the maximum out of 'qualifiers'. Peter was not about to let both riders waste set up time during the race weekend and somebody had to sort out race tyres.

Even so, Carl Fogarty should have won the 1993 championship. Carl won almost twice as many races as Scott that year. Without the consistency of the team effort that kept Scott and me at the front of the field it would have been a different story. But late in the season Carl had cracked under the pressure of his first ride in a factory Ducati team. The wheels came off his title bid in the second race at Sugo. Despite Scott's new engine from the Kawasaki factory, Carl had the race in the palm of his hand. Then he threw it away with a silly passing move on a lapped rider, and was chucked over the handlebars. Just a little more patience and he would have won, and kept the pressure on Scott. It was the turning point in the 1993 title chase.

It also wasn't the only success Kawasaki had in Japan that year. Scott and I made Kawasaki history by scoring the first Suzuka 8-Hour win for the brand. It was the last year the 8-Hour adopted the F1 formula, as the organisers were moving to a Superbike one to keep down the costs of racing in Japan's most popular race. It was another victory won by consistency. Honda went all out to win the most important Japanese race of the year at their own circuit; as it was the last time they could race the RVF750 which had dominated the race through the early 1990s. They flew in 500 champs Mick Doohan and Eddie Lawson, and gave them strong teammates in Daryl Beattie and Satoshi Tsujimoto. Yet both Doohan and Lawson crashed at various stages of the race, handing the lead to Scott and me. We just kept on circulating, Peter ensuring the pit stops and strategy were flawless. By the time the chequered flag came out, only Lawson was on the same lap. It was a team victory rather than the result of any individual brilliance, and Peter played no small part in it.

Leaving Kawasaki wasn't easy. Peter and the Aussie team were returning to Australia and Muzzy had a new team manager. I had not been happy with the change to American control of the team in 1993 and felt, with Peter and the boys leaving, it would only get worse. I felt a sense of obligation as the Doyle-led Team Kawasaki Australia outfit was the first big team to recognise my potential, and I was in two minds about accepting the Honda offer. Honda wanted to pay me 75 percent more than Kawasaki, and if I had been in racing just for the money, I would've had few reservations about joining 'Mighty Honda'. But I'd had five good years racing in Kawasaki teams, and it was hard to let go.

Raymond Roche had also offered me a contract with Ducati for even more money than Honda. He'd made the offer in a handwritten fax, but I didn't feel comfortable about the deal, as it wasn't a proper letter of intent. I was lucky not to get my hopes up as the Ducati factory appointed Virginio Ferrari as team manger instead of Roche - and I would have been out on my ear. While chewing over the Honda deal, I asked Peter's father, Neville Doyle - the great team manager and engine tuner who looked after Greg Hansford - for some advice. He outlined the changes at Kawasaki for 1994, and said: "You've got to do it, Aaron, Kawasaki has left you with no choice. Peter's gone now and we feel the team has slipped even further behind."

I also talked to Doug Polen at the cancelled last round of 1993 championship in Mexico. Doug was on the verge of signing with Honda and said an opportunity to ride for them was too good to miss. I was less than convinced, having seen the Honda RC30 slide back through the Superbike fields over the years. I didn't mention Honda in the same tones of reverence most of the paddock seemed to, and I didn't subscribe to the view that this was the best Japanese bike manufacturer to race for. Hadn't we just kicked their butt at Suzuka? But Doug, a two-time World Superbike champion, said in all of his racing experience, he had never seen a bike company with bigger budgets and such a large appetite for racing as Honda. So I signed with the world's largest bike manufacturer.

My first ride on the new RC45 V4 made me wish I hadn't. It was so slow. I yearned for my Kawasaki, but my teammate had an even bigger shock. He had joined Castrol Honda after riding a Fast By Ferrachi Ducati, and crashed down to earth from an even greater height. Doug had been sucked into the whole 'Mighty Honda' thing and had convinced me of the same myth. But 'Mighty Honda' had, it seemed, just produced a "slow piece of shit" to quote my teammate. Judging by the first tests of the RC45, Honda must have grossly underestimated the competition. They had won the first two World Superbike Championships, in 1988 and 1989 with American Fred Merkel, and then concentrated most of their racing resources on Grand Prix. While Honda had put most of their HRC budget into the two-stroke basket, Ducati had worked wonders within the WSC rules, and had lifted the reliability of their machines in Honda's absence. Doug was totally detuned from the first ride. Was this really Honda's 'Great White Hope' for World Superbike success?

We tested the thing everywhere before the first race of the 1994 season. We tested at Donington twice, Eastern Creek, Suzuka, Pembrey, and at

Phillip Island with all the Honda Racing Corporation crew. At the Island, I was almost two seconds off my World Superbike lap record, but Doug was even slower. His times were 2.3 seconds slower than mine, so he was 4.2 seconds off a competitive time. He was in back-marker territory. Things were getting desperate on the bike development front with the first race of the WSC calendar fast approaching.

While the bike needed work, the Castrol Honda team was shaping up well. Adrian joined as my chief mechanic, and a little later on, as replacement for Phil Baldwin, he had the back up of fellow Kiwi Norris Farrow, the ex-racer who had guided Fred Merkel to his two WSC titles on the Honda RC30. My other two mechanics were Ian Richards and Richard Myers. It was a new, inexperienced team, so I knew how important it was to gather the right people around me. I obtained the services of Adrian and Norris to ensure we would be strong enough to take our own direction. As it turned out, our strength would lead the team in many aspects. We had all had world championship experience and knew what it took to win. This began to influence the team's structure, and I believe our efforts over the years made Castrol Honda the team it is today.

However, Adrian aside, that influence and leadership has waned since 2000. Looking from the outside, the 2001 team has let its guard down. The inherent problems of the 2000 machine are still visible in 2001, and with tougher competition, it was always going to be a struggle for Colin Edwards to retain the title.

Harvey Beltran looked after team logistics. However there was much more to Harvey than running around organising everybody. He was a jack-of-all-trades, and seemed to know somebody everywhere. Every team needs a Harvey. Ours became a very close and personal friend as well. He always kept his sense of humour, and his easy smile at the end of a hard day would make all the difference. At times, Harvey played practical jokes on the team management to relieve the tension. My favourite was the "the 6 cm cockroach".

Neil Tuxworth, the team manager was the butt of many of Harvey's jokes. He was afraid of bugs and creepy-crawlies, and there were plenty in Indonesia, all begging for new homes. So Harvey put a cockroach in Neil's suitcase. Neil found it one morning, and began screaming and yelling, while trying to flick it out. Harvey came to Neil's aid, his deviant mind springing into action. The bug was now dead, and Harvey got out the twink bottle and wrote "Hi Neil" on its back. He then filed it away neatly in Neil's briefcase, which he would open again about five hours later at the circuit. We had a good laugh waiting for Neil to open his briefcase that day.

Neil was a nice guy, perhaps a little too nice for such a role. He was a good negotiator, supportive of his riders, fair at all times, and knew where every pound of the team's budget was being spent, and why. But he lacked the hard-headed attitude of a Peter Doyle. During my seven years with Castrol Honda, there would be a few occasions when Neil would accept things Peter wouldn't have put up with. He'd shy away from confrontation, where Peter would've stopped the bullshit dead in its tracks. Neil's first great test as team manager happened at our very first World Superbike race together. He did his best, but the situation needed more than that.

However, there was no denying Neil's sense of fairness, and for the first time as a factory rider I felt I was being treated as an equal to my teammate. My two bikes were named A S 1 and A S 2, while Doug's were D P 1 and D P 2 to make the point there was no number one or two riders. In those early days of developing and sorting out the RC45 there were lots of updated parts coming through from HRC, but we always got them at the same time. Neil introduced the practice of extended post-race and post-test debriefings, and these became a hallmark of the Castrol Honda team until John Kocinski came along. The press got a bit miffed by these meetings. Nobody could get hold of Honda's riders after practice or races, as we'd be trying to reinvent the wheel at the end of each day.

At these sessions, the riders, chief mechanics, Neil, and the HRC staff attached to the team tried to nut out ways of getting more performance out of the RC45. The Honda would later become notorious on the WSC circuit for its understeer - its willingness to push straight ahead under power instead of turning - but that only surfaced once we got the engine up to speed. By the first race of the 1994 season, at Donington, we were still concerned by a lack of power. The fuel-injected 750 cc V4 engine was way down on power, and we used short gearing, and a quick shifter to change gear, to help stay on the pace. The closer spacing between the gear ratios enabled us to keep the V4 in its narrow band of top-end power at all times, while the quick shift gave us the ability to shift mid-corner without losing momentum. Being able to shift in places where conventional bikes couldn't, like the Donington chicane, improved our lap times by half a second. We might not have had power of other competitors, but we were determined to put what little we had to the track at every opportunity.

It was a powertrain strategy that almost worked at the very first World Superbike race. I finished second to Carl Fogarty on the equally new Ducati 916 at the first of two Donington rounds. The whole team was ecstatic as we were expecting the worst given our pre-season testing. We hadn't made the test times public, so the whole 'Mighty Honda' myth went unchallenged. The Emperor wasn't revealed as having no clothes. The press and the fans really did not know just how much behind the eight ball we were. By contrast, Ducati turned up at the first round with virtually no testing and won.

Doug was 9th in his first outing on the RC45, and Simon Crafar was the second Honda home, bringing the privateer Rumi bike home in 6th, while Scotsman Brian Morrison was another Honda mounted rider to beat the former double world champ. I was pleased with the debut on the RC45, as second place was beyond my wildest dreams during testing. Yet the elation was short-lived. Before the second race, the officials sprang an impromptu fuel test, and Andy Meklau's 888 Duke and my Honda were the only bikes singled out.

Our fuel was found to be illegal, and Meklau and I had our points from Donington stripped away. The fuel test had shown higher levels of the additive diene than those permitted by a seven-year-old limit in the rules. Our fuel supplier Elf apologised for the mistakes in their brew, absolving both teams of any blame. Elf had supplied teams with the same fuel they formulated for the 500 Grand Prix paddock, thinking that Superbike was under the same regulations. They also told the FIM (Federation of International Motorcycle Racing) officials most other teams had also used the same fuel, so there was no way the Honda or Ducati had gained any advantage from the increased levels of diene.

Although just about everyone was racing on the same fuel, Meklau's bike and my Honda were the only ones tested, and we were the only riders penalised that day. Yet the Elf appeal to the FIM to show prudence in the matter fell on deaf ears. The rest of the 1994 season would be upset by a series of to-and-fro judgments on the issue. At one round I'd have my Donington points back and thanks, mainly to a string of second places through the season, I'd lead the points table. Then next round, I'd have them stripped away again, and I'd slide back behind Carl and Scott in the title race.

It was a farce of sit-com proportions. It may have been a dumb decision to penalise two riders for using the same fuel as everyone else, but I also blame Honda and Neil for not sorting it out at the beginning. The FIM didn't allowing any more appeals from Honda, but they were willing to squash all my fines and cover the team's legal costs. This, to me, says that the FIM saw our innocence and tried to make amends with Honda while favouring Ducati's protest over the matter. Neil had bought a new era of professionalism to the paddock, and lifted World Superbike's image almost to Grand Prix levels. A little more leverage applied to the FIM might have nipped the controversy in the bud, and allowed the team to get on with the real business of winning races without having to wonder, "what's our points total this week?" at the following rounds. We were always aiming at a shifting goalpost in 1994.

Meanwhile Doug was in the doldrums. Stories appeared in the press that this was the way things were meant to be. They portrayed Doug as the more experienced and technical of Castrol Honda's two riders; I was the Wild Colonial Boy who could ride around the RC45's shortcomings. I was happy to accept the comment about my riding being able to overcome the deficiency in the machine, and I'm glad HRC eventually acknowledged the role my mechanics and I played in creating a world-beater out of the RC45. It was just like the previous year - my team mates grew to like my settings for the bike more than their own.

There were three riders chasing the 1994 title - Carl, Scott, and me - then plenty of daylight to Doug. He showed some form in the second race of the second round at Hockenheim. In the first, Scott and I had cleared out from the rest of the field, and I kept the RC45 in the slipstream of the faster Kawasaki. Scott had towed me to second place; he'd leave me behind down the straights through the top three gears, then I'd catch up again at the chicanes. In the second race, the same thing happened, only Doug and Ducati rider Fabrizio Pirovano were now in the draft as well. With a few laps to go, I was just working out my last lap strategy, when the V4 engine locked up. I was back-shifting into turn one when it locked up. The Honda did a U-turn, and then fired me off backwards, towards the crowd. I then had to tell everyone I crashed out, because Honda were quite sensitive about engine failures in those days. Their bikes always officially expired because of "electrical problems". If, in fact, a stray conrod had chopped the engine in half, and maybe knocked the alternator off, it caused an "electrical problem". This time rider error got the blame. I understood Honda's sensitivity at the time - it was a new bike, after all. Problems were almost always caused by a faulty batch of replacement parts.

Doug went on to finish third in that race, and he secured a place on the rostrum another two times with a pair of thirds at Zeltweg, Austria. But those were to be the highlights of his World Superbike career with Honda, and he was a shadow of the force who had won 17 races from 24 starts when winning the 1991 World Superbike title with Ducati. Perhaps his fondest Castrol Honda memory was our 1994 Suzuka 8-Hour win.

It was the closest race in the 17 year history of the event. Once again Honda put on a show of force, with no less that five factory RC45s on the start line. Once again Scott had gone fast to qualify the Kawasaki on pole, and I eyeballed him from third place on the grid as we waited for the start. It was to be an eight hour-long battle, me versus Scott, then I'd hand over to Doug, and he'd continue the battle against Terry Rymer, Scott's teammate. Scott and I were the hares of each team. We'd get close to our qualifying times as we did battle that day, with Scott a little slower than his, and me faster than mine. Meanwhile, Terry and Doug had their own war, but at a slightly slower pace. Apart from times when one of the bikes was in the pits, the factory Kawasaki and Honda were never more than a few seconds apart. As dusk fell, the odds started to tip in our favour.

The RC45 had the advantage of self-adjusting fuel injection, while the Kawasaki used carburettors. In the 8-Hour, each bike must be able to do one hour on a tank of gas, so the bikes have to run 'real lean' to go the distance. As dusk fell, and the air became more dense and loaded with oxygen, the Kawasaki started to lose its edge, the extra oxygen making the mixture even leaner. Meanwhile, the more sophisticated electronics of the Honda adjusted the fuel/air mixture settings automatically to the conditions and, by the last hour, the bike was running better than ever.

To take advantage of this, the team decided to cut Doug's last stint short to maximise my time on the bike. He'd set us up well with a clinical pass on Rymer after we'd sent him out on soft tyres with a short fuel load.

But Doug's times were in the 2m 14 second range, where I could regularly run 2m 12s. As soon as we swapped, the Kawasaki crew were onto our strategy, and quickly swapped Rymer for Russell. I was feeling pretty cocky as I swept by Scott as he exited the pits, so I gave him the 'bye-bye' hand gesture. It was probably the worst thing I could have done, because he put his head down and came charging after me.

It started to get dark, and my RC45 became a shadow illuminated in the lights of the chasing Kawasaki. I held the racing line, and held it fast, to try to force Scott into going the long way around me. During the last 50 minutes of the race, we must have passed every other bike on the track. Sometimes I'd charge up the inside of the back-marker, and he'd follow me through, sometimes we'd blitz by the slower bike, one on each side. There was no quarter asked, and none given, both of us determined to win two Suzukas in a row. With 17 minutes of the race to run, Scott dived through on the inside of the fast left-hander leading off the back straight, but I wasn't having any of that. I immediately re-passed him on the brakes leading to the final chicane, and cut loose. I had qualified with a time of 2m 12.831 seconds, but started clocking in the low 2m 12s in the charge to the flag. Scott responded, dipping to a mid 2m 12s at one stage. And this was in the dark, on shagged tyres, with plenty of lappers getting in our way.

No photograph would really capture the close nature of the RC45's first world series win (the 8-Hour was a round of the World Endurance Championship), for it was completely dark by the time the chequered flag fell. I crossed the line 0.289 of a second in front of Scott, as the crowd celebrated the closest 8-Hour race ever. No longer was the RC45 the paddock bridesmaid, no longer was I to play second fiddle to any other team rider. I'd become a motorcycle racing legend in Japan, where hundreds of thousands of Suzuka 8-Hour fans would look back and remember, "I was there in 1994 for the great Honda versus Kawasaki battle".

If the fans were happy, so were Scott and I. I was absolutely ecstatic with the win, and Scott was initially happy with his effort as well as he came down off the thrill of the chase. Then it began to dawn on him he'd lost the race. Lost it by a fraction of a second. His smile faded as the realisation of losing the race sunk in. You don't ride the Suzuka 8-Hour to finish second. Like any other race, you go flat out to win. But finishing second at Suzuka is a huge gut punch psychologically. First is the only position worth it after putting in all that bloody effort.

However, a Superbike Championship is a different beast to a one-off endurance race. Second takes on more importance, because it means a lot of points especially if you string together plenty of second place finishes in a row. In 1994 I felt like a regular visitor to the podium. It seemed like every race, I'd be up there, opening the champagne and spraying the crowd. Or dousing the winner of the race. I didn't win one World Superbike race in '94, yet I was always in contention for the title, courtesy of nine second place finishes, several thirds, and umpteen fourths. If I'd got my 17 Donington points back, I'd have finished second in the title. As it was, I finished third behind Scott, with 277 points to 280. Meanwhile, Carl became Ducati's favourite son, winning the title with 305 points in the debut year of the 916. If my second place at Donington had been counted, I would have led the points table most of the year, and put more pressure on Carl. He had already shown himself to be vulnerable late in the season, by losing the title to Scott the year before.

Doug was totally frustrated, and finished fourth in the championship with 158 points, five points in front of Rumi Honda's Simon Crafar. Doug would not openly admit defeat, but he was obviously frustrated and could not come to grips with the bike. This was apparent by what he wanted changing on the bike. He was upset with the crew working on it, and tried to get some of the people replaced. I had put a lot of attention into getting the right people around me - people whose advice I knew I could trust. Doug hadn't paid as much attention to the make-up of his support crew, and tried to make changes mid-season when most of the technical talent was already spoken for. Support crews are just one of the basics riders should have sorted before the season starts. Anyone who thinks he can just turn up and ride around any problems that may develop because he's a good rider is deluding himself. You have to have the complete package sorted before the flag drops.

So I didn't feel bad about not winning the 1994 Championship, for I had a double world champion to compare my effort with, and I'd finished 130 points in front of him. Our bikes were identical in their technology, but I suspect the real difference in our performance was largely due to the efforts of Adrian, Norris, and the rest of my crew. That, and attitude. Doug had come from Ducati expecting just as easy a ride from Honda, but quickly found the odds stacked against the 750cc fours. He wasn't the first World Champ to find the RC45 a harder ride than the bigger V-twin he was used to.

Doug probably shouldn't have had such high expectations of Castrol Honda. We were a brand new team with a brand new bike, competing against rules that penalised our chosen engine format. There were a lot of hurdles to overcome from the start.

The challenges of getting the RC45 on the pace made 1994 a satisfying year for me. There would be other years with Honda when I wouldn't feel so pleased with myself, but I was chuffed with how the year went. There were plenty of times when riding skill made up for the difference in the machinery. At Misano I got a third behind Russell and Falappa, and a fourth behind Falappa, Russell and Lucchiari. Now many might think: what's so great about a third and a fourth instead of two wins? But each time I beat a strong Ducati factory bike for the position. In the first race it was Stephane Mertens whose red bike would pull the stickers off the RC45 as it hurtled by around the long left hander leading onto the back straight. In the second it was Carl Fogarty's. Yet I'd be all over them in the corners, eventually passing them. At the one race in Indonesia, I nearly gave the RC45 its inaugural World Superbike win, but Jamie Whitlam's 916 was just too fast off the Sentul circuit's corners. I beat the rest of the red brigade that day, though, and took some pride in my role. I was now my own man. I was not being told what to do by a controlling team manager like Peter Doyle. I had previously been forbidden to wheelie as Peter claimed it was 'bad' for the bike. I had now shaken off those shackles and celebrated my racing more on the slow-down lap of each race. I was riding on a high, and no one could convince me I wasn't the best rider on the 1994 grid.

Honda also showed their pleasure with a new contract for the 1995 season that I signed instantly. Ducati were also showing interest, but I didn't want to be the second rider to Carl Fogarty. Carl had been playing mind games in the paddock with me all through 1994. He'd pretend I didn't exist, and refused to talk to me or make any eye contact. If he saw me coming, he'd spin on his heels and walk the other way. It was quite funny at the time, because I'd known the Fogarty family for some years, and had got on well with Carl and Michaela's oldest daughter Daniela. She'd wave out and yell "Hi, Aaron" while her father looked the other way and tried to blot me out of his thoughts.

The friendship Megan and I had with the Fogarty family ended as soon as I became a threat to Carl's 1994 title hopes. He had a strategy of using the press to snipe at his rivals in an effort to demoralise them. In 1993 Scott Russell was the brunt of his bad mouth and antics. In 1994 I was Carl's worst enemy. The press had a field day, and it was a very public battle between Carl and myself both on TV and in the *Motor Cycle News*. Carl had now become the *MCN's* pet puppet and he was willing to have his strings pulled. Scott and I became wary of the press and its obvious favouring of Carl. We became very choosy about who we talked to as our interviews were usually taken out of context.

There were other good reasons for renewing my contract with Honda. The RC45 had progressed throughout the year, and we were going to use Michelin tyres for 1995 - my preferred tyre choice in my Team Kawasaki Australia days. Doug had instigated the use of Dunlops in 1994; he wasn't going to sign with Castrol Honda unless he got the tyres he wanted. So Honda had put their long association with Michelin on hold to ensure they secured the services of a double World Champ for their Superbike team. Now that Doug had failed to fire, Honda were returning to their preferred tyre supplier.

No doubt this tyre decision was weighing heavily on Doug's mind as we gathered for a debrief after a test session in Japan in January 1995. Doug silenced the room by announcing he didn't want to ride for the team anymore. You could have heard a pin drop. Doug was on a two-year contract with Castrol Honda, and wanted out. He didn't want any more humiliation, didn't want to ride the RC45 on Michelins. We had already noticed the effects of the new tyres in the testing. All our changes through 1994 had tailored the bike to the Dunlops, now HRC had suddenly chucked us onto the Michelins without realising it would stall the team's development of the bike. We were going back to square one for 1995.

As Doug outlined a deal that would allow Honda to buy him out of his second year with them, I couldn't believe what was happening before my eyes. Here was a world champion chucking in the towel, and wanting Honda to pay him for doing nothing for them all year. He wanted to take HRC's money and run - back to the States where he could have another easy ride in a Ducati team. I wondered about the morals of it all. Being paid by Honda to race a Ducati? It sounded like madness, yet HRC readily agreed to Doug's terms. They obviously thought they were better off without him.

So Doug went home, and told the press that HRC had sacked him. It was more like he sacked them. It wouldn't be the first time a world champ jumped from the Castrol Honda ship after just one year racing against the all-mighty Ducatis. But now there was the issue of who would take Doug's place. By January everyone with any WSC experience was already locked into a team. So Simon Crafar was the obvious choice. He was contracted to Oscar Rumi's private Honda team, and an alliance was quickly forged. Simon would race Doug's bikes in Rumi livery, the purple and black paint job contrasting strongly with the red, white, and green of Castrol's colours. There would be Castrol stickers placed on the bikes to keep the sponsor happy.

Doug wasn't the only four-cylinder rider to escape Ducati's dominance in World Superbike that year. Scott Russell abandoned the Muzzy Kawasaki team as well, replacing Kevin Schwantz in the Lucky Strike Suzuki 500 team. Scott left it until after the first three WSC rounds of the 1995 season to advise Muzzy of his intentions. He even said, when he turned up at Donington for what proved to be his last WSC races, an injured foot sustained during testing of the Suzuki 500 was the result of a mountain bike accident. So how did Scott squirm out of Muzzy's contract? He invoked a clause that said Muzzy must provide him with competitive machinery, and then proved the Kawasaki ZXR750R was no match for the Ducati 916.

Despite being a happy traveller in the Castrol Honda camp, I was a little envious of Scott's 500 ride. Earlier that year, during three days of testing at Phillip Island with the Grand Prix teams, I was given the opportunity to ride the Honda NSR500 on the final afternoon. All Honda's 500 GP crew were there - Mick Doohan, Alex Criville, Loris Capirossi, and Shinichi Itoh. They had been testing the 500 for three days, and I got to do around 40 laps on my dream machine. It was awesome. Compared with a Superbike, a 500 two-stroke is a different kind of animal. There's a lot more feedback from the bike compared with a production chassis and, to me, it was easier to find the limit on a 500. The GP bike also turned so much more quickly than the Superbike in Phillip Island's faster corners. It felt like it was on rails. I only had a couple of hours to set the bike up and cut a 1m 35.9 second lap to Itoh's best of a 1m 36.5. My fastest lap was around two seconds off Doohan's best, and 0.4 of a second behind Criville and Capirossi, but I was happy with that, given my limited experience on a 500, and the lack of time to set it up.

I thought I did everything right in front of the HRC bosses that day. I hadn't chucked their bike away like many riders upon first encounter with a 500, and I'd beaten the times of some of their GP regulars. I hoped the potential I showed would lead to a Grand Prix ride, and looked forward to riding a 500 again. In 1995, the Superbike series was on the up at a time when attendances at Grand Prix races were dropping. The WSC rounds in Germany, England, and Holland were starting to draw crowds of up to 50,000 spectators, and these days a British round will draw over 120,000. But like just about every other rider of the mid-1990s I wanted to ride a 500 - a proper purpose-built race bike instead of something derived from a production machine. But first I wanted to win the World Superbike Championship for Honda, then get ushered, as the WSC hero, into their Grand Prix team.

So I forgot the 500 dream, and got on with the job at hand. No two Superbike teams racked up more test miles than Castrol Honda and the Virginio Ferrari-led Ducati squad in the lead-up to the 1995 season. We had received a big motor upgrade, and were now sorting our eighth new engine. The V4 also sported a new 4-into-2 exhaust system. There was more mid-range and top-end power, but now the chassis became our main concern. The extra power resulted in more understeer when powering off the turns, and we were having problems adapting the chassis to the Michelin tyres. These were making the bike unstable; we would struggle all year to find the right compromise between high-speed stability and tuning out the understeer. Through '94, Michelin had been concentrating on V-twin 1000s and now had to change their tyre development to also incorporate the different power characteristics of the RC45. For the Ferrari-managed Ducati squad of Fogarty and Mauro Lucchiari, tyres weren't such an issue. They could call on all their success with the 916 in 1994, as they were using the same Michelin tyres again, and had my old Swann Series mate Anders Anderson helping them set up their Ohlins suspension.

Brakes weren't the issue for the lighter Ducati that they were for us. To make Superbike racing more affordable, the FIM banned carbon discs, and forced us all to use steels. This was a major blow to the Japanese bike teams, as braking was where we tended to make up ground on the red bikes. Kawasaki and Honda complained long and hard about the issue, as it affected heavier bikes more than the lighter twins. It seemed a mockery to claim this move, saving a team around $10,000 on a set of front discs, would make the racing more affordable when it was known the Ducati 916 needed new crankcases after just about every round.

So Honda's back was firmly against the wall as the 1995 season started. There was the adverse publicity about Doug's 'sacking', the brake fiasco, and the tyre change to get used to. The FIM would eventually relax the minimum weight rules, upping it for the twins while lowering it for the fours, to bring the two engine formats within five kgs of each other. However, the rule change didn't occur until half way through the season, and had little influence on the results. For me the big issue about World Superbike rules had always been the larger engine size the twins were allowed. Instead of just four 916 factory Ducatis on the 1995 grid, there were now a host of 'Fogarty replicas' as well - some in the hands of good riders such as Pier Francesco Chili and Fabrizio Pirovano. And it was known that some of these private teams were taking their engines out to the maximum 1000cc permitted by WSC rules.

The Fogarty-Ferrari-Ducati-Michelin combination was tough to beat in 1995. With the help of Anthony 'Slick' Bass on the spanners, and Anders on the suspension, Carl won 13 WSC races from 24 starts. There were few opportunities to rain on his parade at the front of the field. At Albacete, I gave the RC45 its first World Superbike win, much to the relief of the team. It had been a long, hard 18 months coming, and it wasn't through a lack of trying. I was recognised as the most committed rider in the paddock, and we were convinced our team were the hardest workers. Where the factory Ducati guys would enjoy red wine and pasta at lunch, my guys would be lucky to grab a pork pie and a Coke on the run. It was no surprise that the break-through happened at Albacete, one of my favourite tracks. It's a bit like racing back at Manfield - stop, start, stop, start - all the way through a lap.

The second win of the year came at the Sentul circuit in Indonesia. I remember thinking as I turned the last corner and wheeled the bike towards the chequered flag, that "at last we're on the right track". The bike was finally sorted with just one round of the 1995 season to go. I had closed the gap to Ducati rider Troy Corser, in second place on the points table, to just eight points, and was looking forward to scrapping with him at Phillip Island for the runner-up position. But, for me, the victory celebrations were short-lived.

It was at Phillip Island, that Neil Tuxworth told me Carl Fogarty would be my teammate the following year.

eight

No Replacement for Displacement

Why did Carl Fogarty limit his chances of winning a third World Superbike title in a row by exchanging the all-conquering factory Ducati for a 750cc Honda? Perhaps Carl was baited into the move by my constant criticism of the rules. Perhaps he thought: "I'm the great Foggy and I'll show them I can win on anything." Perhaps it was simply that Honda money was worth more than Ducati money, that the exchange rate was better for the yen than the lira. Whatever. Carl soon found out in 1996 that it doesn't matter how good a rider you are. There's simply no replacement for displacement.

One only has to look at the statistics for proof. Out of seven manufacturers, Ducati have won roughly 75 percent of the World Superbike races held so far. That leaves 25 percent for six different manufacturers to share. The crumbs were picked up by Kawasaki, Yamaha, Suzuki, Honda, Bimota and Aprilia. Hard to argue with those kinds of statistics, don't you think? During the 1990s, they won the championship every year but two. That's an 80 percent strike rate for one of the smallest motorcycle manufacturers in the world. For quite a few years the rules were totally stacked in their favour and, as a maker of twin cylinder engines, they still enjoy a 33 percent cubic capacity advantage over the fours. Then there's the fact that Ducati didn't have to build as many bikes for homologation - the World Superbike rule that states how many units of a particular model need to be made before it can race in the production based series. Japanese manufacturers had to build 1000 bikes before their contender was eligible to race in the series while smaller manufacturers like Ducati needed to build a fraction of this number. So they could build thinly disguised race bikes without the need to build commercially viable road bikes on which to base their Superbike campaigns.

While Ducati was still owned by the Castiglioni family, they started working on their own 750cc four, supposedly with the help of Ferrari. When it finally emerged that bike was the MV Agusta F4. It was never raced. There simply was no need to when the Superbike rules so favoured the twins.

Ducati gradually lost their weight advantage over the 1990s as the World Superbike organisers realised the dominance of the red bikes was bad for the sport, but it was a long time coming. At the start of the last decade of the 20th Century, the weight handicap applied to the fours was 25 kilograms. According to ex-racer Steve McLoughlin, one of the men who first drew up the rules, it had been intended to apply a 25-pound penalty to the 750cc fours, and that was what the FIM agreed to. Somehow the weight difference got changed to 25 kilograms when the rules were drafted and, although Honda originally won the first two championships with the RC30, Ducati quickly began to build bikes that were virtually unbeatable over a long and varied season. I don't know why the Japanese manufacturers put up with this formula. They could have united and used their power to push Ducati into using their 750 four. Instead, the Japanese manufacturers are now starting to build twins to be competitive.

The World Supersport capacities also make me laugh, as they are 600cc four cylinders and 750cc twins. A 750 twin is only 25 percent bigger than a 600 four so if Ducati had made a 800 they could have argued that it was the same formula as World Superbike - the twin 33 percent bigger. There is no rhyme or reason to the FIM's formulas. So, who knows what is going to happen with new GP1 rules? The first drafts are way too complicated to sort out who is actually the best rider.

There were rumours that the Ducati factory started encouraging privateers racing their bikes to stay away from the World Series. They were embarrassed that these private teams could potentially beat the factory 750cc fours, and were worried a complete sweep of the top 10 positions in a Superbike race might force the FIM to take away their engine capacity advantage. So some said that several Ducati teams were encouraged to stay home, and race in their respective national championships. With the extra engine capacity, a Ducati V-twin generates around 30 percent more torque than a 750cc four. Peak power might be similar, but it's this extra grunt that really makes the difference. Can you imagine any other motorsport code allowing a 30 percent torque advantage to one engine over another? Imagine NASCAR saying to Ford that the Taurus stock car can have 30 percent more torque than the Chevy Monte Carlo. Don't you think Chevy would quickly throw in the towel and go home? And the fans as well, for one make dominating a series takes a lot of interest away.

Although World Superbike kept growing through the 1990s, a lot of that growth was due to Japanese bike manufacturers who stayed committed to a formula that wasn't doing them any favours. By association, the growth was also due to the riders the Japanese teams employed, who often could make a difference at a particular track on a particular day, and 20 percent of the time - even win the entire series. That 20 percent had to be shared by the four Japanese manufacturers during the '90s. A five percent chance for each one of them of winning the championship.

Over the years some riders decided to give the red bikes a go as the grass always looked greener. Their results always improved on the big twin. Some of us were just as stubborn as the Japanese to our own detriment. I found beating Ducati was far more satisfying than joining them. Looking back, I am sure I 'cut my nose off to spite my face' by turning down some great Ducati offers.

These issues were far from my mind at the end of the 1995 season. The disappointment of losing the title didn't last long. Megan and I headed back to New Zealand after the final Australian round to get married in Wellington; she had been planning the big event for what seemed like all year. The service was held in the chapel of Erskine College, her old boarding school. Rob and Carol Phillis flew in for the event, Rob to be my best man, and Carol to be Megan's matron of honour. The honeymoon machine was the Harley-Davidson Fat Boy I kept in New Zealand for the odd times I was able to get back. I'd bought it because I didn't want to go fast on the road, but it was a shock to find just how slow 'the Great American machine' was.

So I made sure that, before collecting my new bike, Wellington Motorcycles had put a S&S stroker kit in it, to give it a little extra horsepower. This workshop had worked wonders on the Suzukis Robert Holden and Bob Toomey raced against me. Soon the Harley was up to the pit lane speed to which I was accustomed.

Megan and I took off on a honeymoon tour of the South Island with another couple - Michael and Clare Weeks - on their bike. Each person was allowed only one saddlebag of luggage. I filled mine with my running shoes, and Megan would never find her saddlebag big enough. We had a fantastic ride. Summer in the South Island is a special time. The native rain forest turns red with blossom, and the West Coast offers one of the most spectacular highways in the world, dissecting the thin strip of land between the Tasman Sea and the highest mountains in New Zealand. One day, Megan and I will do this ride all over again...

The honeymoon was over all too quickly, and it was time to focus on a new season, and the challenge of a new teammate. It was quite a coup for Neil to sign Carl. We were a British-based team, and now we were getting the nation's highest profile rider. Honda's star was rising higher in a land where it was the market-leader. Neil chased Carl hard. They had known each other for a long time, and no doubt Neil sold Carl on just how good the RC45 now was. Carl had always sworn that the Honda was "the fastest bike on the track - just look at the speed traps". Sometimes I wonder about a lot of people and their understanding of speed traps. The speed traps were usually placed for registering car top speeds, so on a bike you were already on the brakes. All the speeds recorded by my RC45 proved was that I was later getting off the throttle and on to the brakes.

By the last round of 1995 at Phillip Island, the rumours about Carl joining Castrol Honda were starting to surface. The official announcement would come later, but by the end of the racing we knew what was going to happen next season. Michaela Fogarty came to see us and said: "Let's put it all behind us, we've got to work as a team."

It was a good sentiment, but it would have been even better if it had come from Carl himself. Not that Carl would ever open up in that sort of way. He'd probably consider it some form of weakness to be the first person to extend the hand of friendship. But it was too late for any such pleasantries between Carl and me. Thanks to Michaela's offer to bury the hatchet, Carl and I would establish a working relationship within the Castrol Honda camp, but that was as far as things went. It was like two lawyers talking to each other only when in court. We weren't rude to each other, but we weren't friends either. He'd burned too many bridges.

Ducati had another ace up their sleeve to counter Carl's defection to Honda. John Kocinski, the 1990 World 250cc Grand Prix champion, was to ride for Virginio Ferrari's factory squad. Kocinski was known to be hard to get along with, and his obsessive-compulsive habits were legendary. Was this the real reason Carl was keen to leave the red brigade?

The other factory Ducati squad was the Promoter team with Australian rider Troy Corser. I didn't rate Troy at the time, as he'd proved easy to beat back in Australia. Now, on a Ducati, he would become my greatest rival during the 1996 season. Also that year, Neil Hodgson was to partner John Kocinski in the factory Ducati team. He would later ride a Kawasaki with a lot less success.

Few eyes were on Troy and me as we lined up for the first 1996 race at Misano. All the pre-season hype focused on Kocinski's and Fogarty's moves, and they were expected to be the Ducati and Honda riders most likely to battle for the title. Kocinski lived up to his 'star' billing in the first round - he won both races, but it was all downhill for him from there. The wheels started coming off as soon as the series moved to tracks that weren't in the Ducati test schedule. The laid-back atmosphere of his team evidently disgusted him, and by mid-season he had stopped talking to his mechanics and team manager Ferrari. John should really have stayed in America.

Corser soon emerged as Ducati's great hope. He'd followed John-boy home in both Misano races, but at the next round at Donington, he really made his mark. He took pole with a lap time that smashed the overall track record, slicing half a second off the time set by Kevin Schwantz on the factory 500 Suzuki in 1991. But he didn't get it all his own way in the races. In the first he cleared out, while I took part in a huge battle for second with four other riders. But I ran off at the Craner Curves after the rear tyre cried enough, and rejoined the track to finish fifth. In the second race, not only could I stay with Troy, I led the race for nine laps before the Michelins went off in the closing stages, and I had to settle for second. The margin was 0.69 as I struggled for traction in the final laps.

And where was Carl while all this was going on in front of his home crowd? He finished 8th in the first race, and 7th in the second. He started complaining in the press that the RC45 didn't suit his riding style. I remember thinking: "Well, it doesn't suit my style either Carl, but it's the bike we're paid to ride, so let's stop moaning and get on with it." His biggest beef with the Honda was what he thought was a lack of corner speed. Carl likes to think he carries more corner speed than anyone else on the track. This inflated view of his own riding skill had something to do with the bike he'd ridden the previous four years - 'the red bike'. But the harder anyone tried with the RC45, the more it would understeer. The front end would push if you tried to flick it harder into the turns. Then you'd get on the gas nice and early, and it would push again. It was just business as usual on the heavier fours. Carl was used to the narrower, lighter 1995 Ducati, which would hold a tighter line through the turns, both going in on the brakes, and out again on the power. I felt like saying, "Welcome to the world of racing 750cc fours" every time I heard him complaining. He now also had to put up with wheel spin for the first time as a Ducati had so much torque it would just jump off the turns.

Out of the 24 races of the 1996 season, I beat him 15 times, and he beat me nine. He brags that he won more races than me in 1996, and I don't deny him that. It's just that the times I beat him, he was nowhere to be seen, and the few times he beat me, I was right behind him - trying to get by.

Corser's early form evaporated in the third round at Hockenheim, and he crashed out of both races. I won the first race, after an unfortunate collision on the last lap with pole-sitter Frankie Chili in the Sachscurve - the infamous left-hander heading towards the chequered flag where so many of Hockenheim's battles are decided. I had put the RC45 up the inside of the Ducati through the turn, stealing the racing line away. Chili didn't back off, and we touched on the exit. I didn't realise Frankie had tumbled into the gravel-trap until after the race. I was surprised to find he wasn't right behind me at the flag.

I was apologetic and taken aback when Frankie proceeded to angrily blame me for my move. But after viewing the video replay, he realised it was a racing incident and that nobody was to blame.

Carl finished fifth in that first Hockenheim race, and was probably still annoyed by the sacking of his chief mechanic 'Slick' Bass in the week prior to the German round. Slick's a great guy, but he didn't fit in with the strong work ethic at Castrol Honda, and Neil had given him his marching orders. So Carl was sitting eating lunch in our pit between the two Hockenheim races, focussing on his RC45, and trying to mentally turn it into a Ducati. Then the mechanics wheeled my bike past him, and he noticed how high the tail section was, noticed the different rear ride height. He then got his new chief mechanic to go over the data acquisition computers and download all my telemetry readings, and these confirmed I was carrying extra speed into the corners, because my bike was steering quicker than his. So he set up his bike to my settings for the second race. It was typical of the one-sided flow of information that year. Only one factory RC45 rider's intellectual property was worth having. There was never anything about Carl's bikes that I desired for mine.

So Carl came back and won the second race at Hockenheim. Suddenly he's the big hero again for having overcome Slick's sacking. I finished one tenth of a second behind him in second place after winning the first race, yet suddenly he's the one all covered in glory. He's the one robbing my points by using my bike set-up. There's no doubt in my mind that if Neil had let me keep my information to myself in 1996, I would have won the championship for Honda. Another five points at Hockenheim, another five the following weekend at Monza - where Carl beat me in the first race by six-tenths. It all would have added up to more pressure on Troy and the Ducati team, and maybe a world title. I left Monza with two seconds in the points bag after two narrow misses on the win. In the second race, Frankie Chili took his revenge for Hockenheim race one, beating me by 0.007 of a second.

My consistency kept me at the top of the World Superbike points table through most of the 1996 season. But a violent crash at the Suzuka 8-Hour took the edge off my riding mid-season. I did the usual crash landing on my feet, and broke two toes, while leading the race, after qualifying on pole. The 8-Hour always added extra pressure and always fell in the middle of the world Superbike season, a crucial time. I think the Japanese thought more of this race than the World Championship. As well as the race, we would do three tests, preparing for the 8-Hour, during the race season. Ducati riders never participated so they got to holiday, with time to recover mid season. I soldiered on, and five days after returning from Japan, I raced in the World Superbike round at Brands Hatch, in the UK because I was only four points behind in the championship and was the lead Honda rider. Carl Fogarty or no Carl Fogarty, I was determined to be Honda's best hope of winning the title.

The Suzuka 8-Hour crash was all the more of a disappointment as it ended my run of wins in the event. I had set a new record for wins in a row, when I won with Tadayuki Okada in 1995. It was the third win in a row, and it happened after a practice crash left me awake all night with my hands in ice buckets. Wayne Gardner is still the only rider to have won the 8-Hour four times, but his wins were more scattered than mine.

The crash in 1996 not only took away my chance of equalling his overall wins record, but any chance of extending the wins-in-a-row record. Not that I think it is a record that will be beaten easily. The Suzuka 8-Hour might not be the longest race in the World Endurance Championship, but it rates as one of the toughest. There's the pace - it's a full-throttle sprint from start to finish. Then there's the conditions - in July, the track temperature is in the 40s, sometimes 50s, degrees Celsius, the humidity in the high nineties. To survive the best teams have restoration pools for their riders, and put them on re-hydration drips between sessions on the bike. You spend half the race going flat out on a motorcycle, the other half in some sort of intensive care hospital. It's not the sort of event that encourages anyone to come back and win again and again.

Yet despite the injuries I was carrying, neither Carl nor Troy pressed home any real advantage. Apart from Assen - Carl's favourite track - I beat my teammate home most of the time. And the Ducati-mounted contender proved to be better at securing pole position than winning races. Chili and Kocinski were just as likely to bring the red bike home first. With two rounds to go, I still held the championship lead by seven points from Troy, and had a 22-point gap on Carl, and 29 points on Kocinski. The last two rounds were at places I enjoyed - Albacete and Phillip Island - so I was reasonably confident of winning.

But it was hard to concentrate on the goal with my team in so much turmoil. By mid-season Kocinski had burned up all his goodwill at Ducati, and Virginio Ferrari was desperate to get rid of him. Ferrari contacted me just before the 9th round of the championship at Sugo to see if I'd be interested in riding the Ducati. He wanted to know the bottom line - how much would it take to get me to switch camps? I wasn't ready to leave Honda as it was a possible ticket to a 500 ride, but I wrote down a figure for him. It turned out to be a ruse to find out the going rate for a Castrol Honda rider. Ferrari was digging around, finding out what he could get me for, and what he could get Carl for. At the next round at Assen, he announced Carl would ride for him in 1997. I couldn't believe Carl would make a public display of jumping ship with three rounds still to go. Was he that desperate to get back on a red bike?

For Honda it was a major embarrassment, and it made my commitment to them look worth its weight in gold. So they were pretty keen to secure me for the following season, and made me a good offer as soon as Ferrari made the Fogarty announcement. Carl mentions the figure he signed for in his book, and I still feel good that my Honda contract showed me I was as sought after as the two-times World Champion.

Between Assen and Albacete, there was a month-long break, so we hung out at the team's base in Louth, Lincolnshire, England and used the local gym to keep fit and focussed. We parked the motorhome up at the team workshop in a dingy English industrial estate. By this time the fifth wheel had gone and we were living in a bus style motorhome, a Holiday Rambler imported from America. We could close the door and forget about our surroundings, amongst all the trimmings of a luxury apartment. I enjoyed being near the team and the bikes. It kept me focused on the job at hand. I just wanted to rest up for the coming battle with Troy for the title. It was then I started to hear rumours about John Kocinski joining the Castrol Honda team. Every day I'd ring Neil to ask, "What's going on? Don't you know how destructive he can be to a team?" Neil stressed there was "no way" John would be joining his team. Then suddenly they signed him, and I thought, "Well, this'll be a challenge." I was getting used to the teammate routine at Honda. Each year, it seemed, they would sign someone they thought would do the business - a world champ or a Grand Prix winner. Each year these guys would want out of their contracts early. It made me all the more determined to win, to show Honda, "Hey, you don't need these guys". A rider has to be committed to keep on scoring points, and Castrol Honda had signed no one more committed to the entire championship than me. But they'd sign these stars, who would fire only some of the time and, although I'd be leading them in the points, they'd steal a race win at crucial times.

Race day at Albacete October 6, 1996, dawned cloudy and cold. The track surface was at a temperature unsuited to the Michelins when fitted to the heavier Honda, and we just couldn't find a tyre that worked. It was like riding on wets. The Michelins did not seem too bad on the Ducatis though. Troy streaked to two race wins, and suddenly grabbed a 26-point lead in the championship. Ducati's homework at Albacete paid off that day. They had conducted test sessions at the Spanish circuit the week earlier, along with Honda and Yamaha. Corser and Kocinski had both smashed the lap record. Their homework was done at my expense. Honda had booked the track for an exclusive test, then Neil decided to share the costs with other teams. Castrol Honda may have saved money, but the move took away any possibility of getting an advantage over the opposition.

While the other teams had rested up, I was sent on a PR mission to the Koln Motorbike Show on the Tuesday and Wednesday before the race. It was madness. On top of that I picked up a bug and had the flu all race weekend. Ironically Carl did not go, as he wouldn't be a Honda man for much longer. Looking back it would have been much better if he had gone to the show and caught the cold and left me to perform to the best of my ability.

In the first race I made the wrong tyre choice. Although nothing seemed to work, it was the best of a bad bunch, and I got swamped in a red and green bike tide, finishing 9th. The second was only a little better, and I finished 6th, just in front of Carl. It was a day that Castrol Honda, and the Michelin liaison people attached to the team, would rather forget.

There was still a faint hope of winning the title at Phillip Island, and I was going to give it my all. I set the fastest laps of both races, but it was all for nought. In the first race I was locked in a battle with Anthony Gobert for the lead. We were really going at it when I lost the front end going into Siberia corner. I was surprised by Gobert's speed that weekend, as he hadn't done much in qualifying. Perhaps he was more fired up by beating me than actually taking the win, as we had had several clashes on and off the track that year. We never saw eye to eye, and were on different wavelengths. My only crash of the 1996 World Superbike season happened on the 13th lap of the race, and it sealed the title for Troy. Although he'd retire in the second race after hitting one of Phillip Island's infamous seagulls, he now had enough points to be crowned world champion. I was determined to make up for it by winning the second race. I chased and caught first race winner Anthony Gobert on the

Paying attention, aged five at Central
School in Masterton, 1971.

Photo: Aaron Slight collection

Right: Making the newspaper pages at
age 14. A photo published in the
Wairarapa Times-Age of me and my
YZ80F motocross bike, at the
Gladstone track. Note the lace-up work
boots and racing numbers made of tape.

Photo: Aaron Slight collection

Last lap. Stealing the racing line, and a win, off Marlboro Yamaha's Peter Goddard while on the Kawasaki superbike in the Mallala round of the 1990 Australian Superbike Championship.

Photo: Andre Kammer

Heading for a Harley honeymoon. Megan and I pose on the Fat Boy while Rob and Carol Phillis look on.

Photo: Martin Stewart

The beginning of the battle. Megan and I look happy and relaxed in this snap from Kylami, South Africa in 1999. Little did we know that pressure was building in the malformed vein inside my brain.

Photo: Aaron Slight collection

Talking shop with Barry. Two-time World 500 champ Sheene pays a visit
to the Castrol Honda pit at Phillip Island in 1997.

Photo: Megan Slight

Previous page: Lucky 13. Racing to victory in my first World Superbike
race on European soil at Albacete, Spain in 1992

Photo: Miguel Harranz

Mohawk man. Another race, and another haircut. My radical
haircuts were a hit with fans, especially in conservative Japan.

Photo: Megan Slight

All smiles in Austria 1998. A double win at the A1 ring was the highlight for me of a troubled yet close fight for the title. Ducati riders Chili and Fogarty were trying to be happy with second best.

Photo: Megan Slight

Home, sweet home. Monaco, playground of the rich and famous, became a European haven for Megan and me.

Photo: Megan Slight

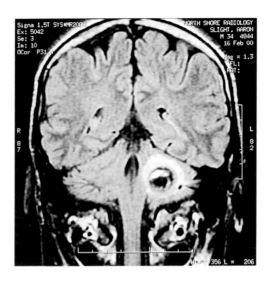

Before: The dark area shows the site of the 2cm bleed inside my head.

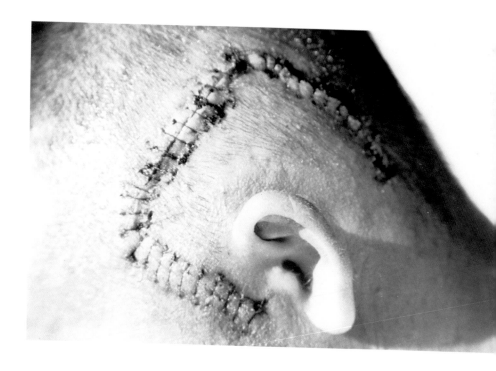

After: Stitched up, after the operation to remove the bleed from my brain.
Photo: Megan Slight

Opposite: Under pressure. I was soon putting pressure on myself after getting back on the bike just 12 weeks after my brain operation in 2000.
Photo: Roger Lohrer

On a big twin, at last. Racing the VTR V-twin at Hockenheim, Germany in one of the last battles with Castrol Honda in 2000.
Photo: Roger Lohrer

This was a moment in my career that will stay with me.
The crowd at Brands Hatch was going crazy as I stripped down
to my underwear in front of thousands. The photos are quite
symbolic but, at the time, I was just expressing my feelings,
which were to rid myself of my Castrol Honda ties. They had
rid themselves of me the night before. It was the end of the
most significant comeback the Superbike scene had ever known
and everyone there that day realised it. It had been most people's
unspoken belief that the chances of me riding again were very
slim. So I left my legacy that day with a boy on the other side
of the Brands Hatch fence. A boy who just happened to be
named Aaron.

Photos: Roger Lohrer

Photo: R Taglibue

Kawasaki, but narrowly lost the race with a wild slide exiting Siberia. The Michelins just did not seem to slide and hook up. The Dunlops were much better at that. The second place gave me the points to finish second in the title, heading off John Kocinski by 10 points. Carl was a further five points behind in fourth.

I felt positive, at the beginning of 1997, that I was headed in the right direction, and in the right team. They'd put another good rider up against me, and I was sure I could overcome the Kocinski challenge as easily as I'd handled Polen and Fogarty. But it went pear-shaped from our very first test together. John simply got up and said that he didn't want to attend the team de-briefings anymore. And suddenly this was OK with Neil. The year before I'd wanted out of the de-briefs just to stymie Carl, and Neil told me "No, you can't do that Aaron, because it's not good for the team." Now Little John was getting away with it. He was manipulating the team's management at the very first test. Neil couldn't put it right because he could not handle a run in with John as John had the Japanese on his side. How he had that support I didn't know. I now knew that 1997 was going to be a struggle, and all the things I had heard about John were coming true. Everybody would try to please him because suddenly everybody was scared of his hot line to HRC.

Then there were the PR obligations. We'd be asked to attend the opening of Honda shops, and I'd drive there. John would fly, and Neil would pick him up from the airport. It was like he had to keep looking after HRC's prize rider. He'd hold his hand, take him to dinner, carry his luggage, anything to keep Mr Kocinski happy. It wasn't just Neil, but the entire team. It became hard to get anything out of them, because they were so busy mucking around babying Little John. John would ensure they had no spare time, as they would be fetching him new air bottles so he could blow out his helmet, clean his gloves, or dry his leathers. John wouldn't put on a spare suit so he had to clean up his favourite kit every day, and he'd distract the team with it all. It really started to get to me. Although he did provide the boys with a few laughs - but behind his back because they didn't want to see John's ugly side. I don't know how he gained this kind of power over people, as he is really just an insecure little man.

The guy has serious problems. Towards the end of 1997 I almost felt sorry for him. But I didn't want to feel sorry for him, because he was starting to beat me in the title. On the track John Kocinski is extremely talented - especially if it's wet. You've got to be talented when you start riding at two; you live with Kenny Roberts and get groomed to be a world champ all through your childhood. John is still the only guy to have won titles in Grand Prix and World Superbike, and that's a unique record. A truly talented rider, but off the track he was a total disaster, a real nut case.

At the first test at Sentul he lapped at the same pace as me. I respected that performance first time on the bike, so I started chatting to him. Give John an inch and he takes 10 miles. He just started talking and talking. It was nothing to do with motorcycles - the subject I really wanted to talk about. He just kept going on and on. It didn't stop - a constant stream of words. All about himself. I talked to Scott Russell about it and he said he just wouldn't get in a car with him again. So every day we took two different taxis to the track and never shared a car again. It was sad as he obviously wanted friendship and was lonely but was also trying to get inside my head and I was not up for it.

He'd wear the same clothes at all 12 rounds of the series. In 1997, it was a HRC T-shirt and orange nylon shorts. Each night I'm sure they were washed to wear again the next day. He never travelled with a suitcase. He'd just get off the plane with his few clothes in a duty-free bag. In the end I asked Kocinski's motorhome driver not to park his rig next to ours. It was just too distracting. I'd end up watching all the craziness.

Like the time it got too cold for shorts, and he had to go put his jeans on. He'd go up the motorhome steps, wiping his feet on each step, take his shoes off, and then open the door using his thumb and index finger. Then he'd come out with the jeans, put his shoes on and shake them round the back of the motorhome for a full five minutes. Shake and shake them to get rid of the bogeymen or whatever. Then he'd go back up the steps, take his shoes off, do the door thing, and go inside and put the jeans on. Then he'd come outside again, doing the same shoe and door ritual to shake the bogeymen out of the shorts he'd been wearing. So it took him forever to do anything. It all got too much for Megan and me. So at the next race meeting I talked with John's motorhome driver and said it would be better if we did not park together. However, John's compulsion to clean did give me a hot tip on cleaning products - Simple Green is amazing. Although I didn't think having a pallet of it on hand was necessary, as John obviously did.

For all his odd behaviour at times, Kocinski was an absolute master of wet tracks. Anytime the heavens opened, he became the bet of the paddock to win. And it rained and rained all through 1997. It was the wettest Superbike season ever. At the first round at Phillip Island, I started the season with a pole position. I went to bed feeling pretty good about the way things were going, and then woke to hear the rain falling heavily on the motel roof. It totally stuffed up the day for me. It didn't stop until just before the first race. Kocinski lead from start to finish on the saturated track, while half the field crashed including yours truly. The next race was a totally different story. The track had dried out by now, and I diced the whole way with Colin Edwards on the emerging Yamaha, and Crafar on the factory Kawasaki - they were both on Dunlops. We'd quickly dropped Fogarty on the Ducati behind, and with two laps to go Colin opened a bit of a gap in front. So I put my head down, and gave it everything. By the last corner I was right up the exhaust pipe of the Yamaha, and the draft from Colin sling-shotted me to the race win. I drafted past just like Mal Campbell had done to me years before, a lesson learnt from the old master. Kocinski finished 7th in the first dry race of the year.

Fogarty was struggling on the factory Ducati and kept complaining how he wanted his 1995 bike, as he couldn't get the 1997 machine to his liking. I don't know any other racer who would rather go back two years in technology than sort out a more powerful, more technically developed machine. It showed how good the bike was in 1995 and it also showed how little Carl knew about setting up a bike. The move to a full 996cc engine had made the Ducati much more difficult to ride. It would be a year that presented the 750cc fours with their best chance of winning since 1993. The YZF750 Yamaha was now also on the pace in the hands of Scott Russell and Edwards, and Kawasaki had made the move of taking the responsibilities of World Superbike off Rob Muzzy and handing them to talented German tuner Harald Eckl. Corser, the one Ducati rider with factory bike experience under the 162 kg minimum weight rule, was having a season racing a private Yamaha 500 with his Promoter team. So the Ducati teams were regrouping, adjusting to a new bike without their most experienced rider. But the great decider in the end was the weather. It eased Kocinski into the seat of the RC45 when it rained and rained through the first three rounds of the championship, and by the time it dried, he'd settled in. With nine victories to John, and three to me, the RC45 would win 12 races out of 24 in 1997. For once Ducati would have to pick up the crumbs.

Kocinski wrapped up the championship at the second-to-last-round at Sugo, in Japan, but there was still second place for the team to race for in Indonesia. I arrived at the Sentul circuit seven points behind Carl, who had won five races to my three. So there was a bit of a team pep talk 10 minutes before the first race, and Neil said John should do everything he could to help Castrol Honda finish 1-2 in the championship. With about five laps left in the race, Kocinski was leading, and I was behind him thinking, "He's trying really hard for someone who's just been told to settle for second." So I decided to pass him anyway, took the lead, and headed for the chequered flag. With two corners to go, Kocinski stuffed his bike up the inside of mine, and deliberately rode me off into the boonies. I had to back off to avoid crashing. I thought he was just proving a point and would slow on the last corner. Yeah right! The wanker just kept his head down and took the chequered flag. I was spitting tacks as I got back to the team pits after the race, and refused to get on the same rostrum with Kocinski. I went off at Neil when he tried to get me up on the rostrum. I told him I thought he was the boss, not John. I said, "Don't you try to force me to go anywhere near that fucking idiot, because I'll punch his lights out."

The potential PR damage of me punching out Kocinski in front of millions of TV viewers was too horrendous for Neil to contemplate, so he backed down on forcing me up on the rostrum. He tried to defend Kocinski, claiming John had been told by HRC to win 10 races that year. I replied, "Oh yeah, when did they tell him that Neil, was it after our pep talk, just a few seconds before the race? Because I didn't see John on the phone!"

Once again, John had made a mockery of the team. It seemed most of the people in charge of the team - both English and Japanese - didn't mind bending over for John. But it just wasn't in my make-up.

Next race the Kocinski kamikaze attack on the last lap happened again, only this time he collided with leader Simon Crafar, and they both tumbled into the gravel trap. In one round of World Superbike, Kocinski had gone from newly crowned champion to total villain. Everyone in the paddock knew that the over-aggressive moves in the two last races of the season were totally uncalled for. He lost the respect of everyone at Sentul, and effectively put his future in any World Championship on ice. Although HRC would give him the 500 ride he craved the following year, it would be a token effort only, and Little John soon high-tailed it back to the good old U.S.A.

nine

If it Wasn't for Bad Luck,
I Wouldn't Have any Luck at All

Between each season I'd think about what I could change to become more competitive. I'd go over every aspect - my personal life, my team, my fitness, my attitude, my riding, and my bike. The 1997 season had made me more determined than ever to win the championship, and I looked at what needed changing to give me a better chance of winning in 1998. I was already going to a sports psychologist, and we worked out that I needed to stop focusing so much on the competition. It was to help me get over the 'But the Ducati is a better bike' thing. Also from that day on I tried to remove the word 'but' from my vocabulary as I believe there is no room for 'buts' - either you can or you can't do something. I knew I could win the title on the 750 as long as I stayed focused on the advantages rather than the disadvantages. 'A Slight Advantage' became my motto for racing, a play on words as the odds were really stacked against us. There were two other missing ingredients that had held me back so far. One was a home - Megan and I needed to settle down somewhere in Europe. The other was a change in my team structure.

Adrian and I had been together for quite a few years now, and the working relationship was getting stale. It had reached a turning point at the 1997 Laguna Seca round. I'd kept asking Adrian for the 1997 test settings as I had gone as fast as John that day. John was now fastest qualifier. I'd come back to the pits after each session and say, "This isn't what we used in the test". This went on all weekend and I was beginning to get frustrated at wasting my test sessions because I couldn't understand why the machine was not being set up as per the test, and my request. Adrian was saying, " Well this bit been's changed since then, and that bit has been modified", and it wasn't easy to get my bike back to the settings I wanted. Excuses I did not want to hear.

Adrian had been great throughout my Superbike career, although some people in the paddock found him hard to deal with. I felt I needed someone who was more positive about me, rather than just strictly technical in all of their support. It was hard to let Adrian go though. He had a huge amount of knowledge on every aspect of the RC45, having been my chief technician with the team since it first raced the Honda V4. I knew that if I opted for someone else the decision to change chief mechanics might come back to haunt me. Adrian would still be contracted to the team, and whoever might replace John Kocinski would quickly benefit from the wealth of experience Adrian and I had accumulated together, from tyre combinations, Dunlop and Michelin, suspension settings, brake set-up, gear-box settings, for each and every circuit over my whole World Superbike career. I would now have to start from scratch. It was time to move on, though, so I asked Norris Farrow to be my chief mechanic.

Then there was the issue of the teammate to sort out. I was keen to see Scott Russell signed. Honda evidently didn't like Scott's attitude, so they signed his Yamaha teammate Colin Edwards instead. He had been due to switch from Superbike to 500s that year, but he held out for too much money and was frozen out of a ride. I rang Colin and suggested he give Honda a call. Honda picked him up on the rebound and, after Kocinski, Colin seemed pleasant and easy-going, for an American.

I also trained harder for 1998. I had finished running on the advice of doctors as it was starting to irritate my lower back. I continued with my swimming and increased my gym work. I started cycling for the first time in my life. The off-season was spent in Wellington. Megan and I rented a place there for a couple of months, and I suddenly had friends to train with. The first time ever, as I had never had personal trainers - motivation was not an issue. However, the competitive nature of the Wellington boys really got me going. Darryn Henderson, a friend from my motocross days, had gone on to become the New Zealand downhill mountain bike champion for a couple of years. He also competed in iron-man events, and he travelled around the world racing downhill for a career. He got me into road cycling. We'd cycle the hills and valleys of the rugged terrain around Wellington. I was fit before, but never as fit as in 1998.

The word "soft" was starting to be included in my vocabulary more and more as I trained with these guys. Although they shaved their legs, they never took the soft option. The Saturday morning 100km ride would be the climax of a great training week. I learnt a lot of techniques from the cycle boys on these Saturday mornings as there were usually about 100 cyclists participating. Techniques on when to save yourself and when to go! This could be applied to tyres in a long race. I soon realised this was one of the hardest sports on earth and these lads did not take to their Lycra lightly. I also think these lads invented road rage, as cyclists aren't respected in New Zealand.

One Friday evening, for example, we were riding around the Wellington harbour and some young lads in their mum's car decided to brake check us while yelling out abuse - "faggots" etc. Immediately we pulled over and stuffed our pockets with stones, then we were off after the lads, as we knew they would be around for some more harassment. This time Darryn let loose with his one and only boulder, which struck the boot of the car. The boys shitted themselves, took off and stopped up the road. As we pulled up, we flicked off our cycle shoes (a little like Reg removing his teeth), to get ready for battle. The boys thought they had the upper hand, as there were more of them, but little did they know that Possum, a six and a half foot tall friend, was peddling back to see what was going on. As I was trying to drag one of the passengers out of the car, the boys spotted Possum, and they were off! We saw them again about 5km up the road, in a phone box, calling the police. So, we cut short our ride that night, and maxed out our hearts taking the back way home.

So, I had a more finely tuned body, a new chief mechanic, and a totally new attitude. All Megan and I needed now was a home. We looked at the options. England was where the team was based, and it had the advantage of speaking our language, but the weather, and the long distance to most of the European races put us off the country many New Zealanders consider their second home. Italy also appealed, but seemed to have some funny rules about foreigners living there. Mick Doohan had always raved about Monaco so, we thought, why not live there?

We sorted out an apartment just around the corner from Mick's, and he and I quickly became training partners. We'd cycle into the hills above the principality, a perfect pairing as we both worked for Honda, but raced in different codes. The rides were very competitive as we egged each other on. Mick introduced me to other motorsport professionals who lived in Monaco. There was Wayne Gardner and David Coulthard, Didier De Radigues, Giancarlo Fisichella and his manager Tarquini. I also lived in the same building as McLaren test driver Alexander Wurz. Alex and I would train a lot together and became good friends. Another nice guy of motorsport.

At last Megan and I had stopped living in the paddock. We still had the motorhome, but now we also had a permanent home. Whenever the racing allowed we could return to Monaco, and live our own life. So now there was just one more ingredient to sort out - the bike.

The Honda was now making good strong top-end power courtesy of a new twin-injector fuel injection system stoking each cylinder. The major problem wasn't going, it was stopping. In 1997 we had experimented with a linked brake system with the aim of improving the way the RC45 turned into corners. The idea was that as the rider braked to the corner apex, a little bit of back brake applied from the front lever would help reduce the understeer. Kocinski had rejected the linked brakes straight away. I kept on trying it, before finally going back to a more conventional system mid-season. Now our Brembo brakes had problems with locking on. It was a real problem in chicanes, where you'd brake for the first turn, then find the brakes dragging through the second. It would destroy a lap time when it happened, not to mention create plenty of potential for a crash. When the 1998 season started, we still hadn't found a solution.

It would take half the year to track it down to the Brembo master cylinder, and Norris and I solved it by secretly using a Nissin master cylinder disguised by a Brembo sticker. The problem may have been exaggerated by the limited movement in my bad hand. I seemed to suffer more "brake drag" than anybody else.

We had to disguise the Nissin master cylinder because of the politics surrounding the brake issue. It took a lot of debate before we were allowed to fit a double-sided swing arm to the RC45 as well. I found the double-sided arm gave a better feel for rear tyre traction, and it was easier on the tyres as well with a minor unsprung weight saving. Yet there were politics getting in the way of our competitiveness again. Honda had paid patent royalties to a French engineer on the single-sided design, and the expense needed justification. Anytime Honda could fit a single-sided swing arm to their racebikes, they did. They used it on the twin-cylinder 250 and 500 Grand Prix bikes and the RC45. Yet strangely, it never appeared on the NSR500 V4 with which Honda secured most of its Grand Prix success.

We also got the stronger handlebars I had been crying out for. Honda engineers had been fitting ultra-light bars, which would just sheer off in a crash, making it impossible to pick up the bike and rejoin the race. I had complained bitterly after the 1996 8-Hour when I crashed the bike and the handlebar had broken off. It took many laps to repair the bike, and it effectively put us out of the race.

The checklist for the 1998 season was complete. We thought we were ready for whatever the championship could throw at us. The weekend before the first race, I checked my fitness with a 56-kilometre mountain bike race. It was the hardest thing I had ever done in my life. I covered the distance over hilly terrain in three hours and 10 minutes. My body was ready like never before. All we needed now was a little help from Lady Luck, the essential ingredient in any winning recipe. Before this season I had believed you made your own luck, now I was about to change my mind.

If it wasn't for bad luck in 1998, I wouldn't have had any luck at all. The final test at Eastern Creek showed I was ready for my strongest bid to win the World Superbike title. I set the fastest time of any four-stroke motorcycle there, just 0.6 of a second slower than Mick on the 500 two-stroke. As for my teammate, I was always confident I could beat Colin, always felt I had the upper hand in his first year on a Honda. When we got to the first round at Phillip Island, I rattled off a 1:34.48 second lap - my fastest ever there. I was fastest in the first official practice session, third fastest in the second, and second in Superpole.

Superpole? It was a new system for determining the grid positions of the top 16 qualifiers. It was supposed to help raise the profile of World Superbike by capturing more TV viewers on the Saturday before the race, but we riders thought it was an abomination. Each rider in the top 16 got one flying lap to really go for it, the shootout shown live on Eurosport. For the riders it was an absolute nightmare. Superbike promoter Maurizio Flammini had obviously not thought it all through and the Superpole rules were changed many times. At this stage they hadn't even decided what would happen if the rain came half way through. I always wanted to do the F1 style qualifying which was a 12 lap maximum for each rider. This would involve the team, pit work, and make it more interesting for the viewers watching strategies unfold. To me, watching one rider doing one lap by himself is not very compelling as he's not about to make mistakes and compromise his starting position. Good work done in official practice could unravel in this circus-like lottery for the final grid positions. The Superpole shootout would be a factor in the 1998 title chase.

Luck deserted me in the first race of the 1998 season. I would go on to win more races than ever before in a single season - five times I stood at the top of the podium, and listened proudly as the New Zealand national anthem played. But I lost the championship by 4.5 points. Four-point-five lousy rotten points. And there were quite a number of races where you could say I lost those four and a half points. You could say I lost them in the very first race, when a lapped rider, Jean-Marc Delatang, picked his bike up mid-corner just as I tried to go around the outside of him. I was left with nowhere to go but onto the grass, where I crashed. I quickly picked up the bike, handlebars intact, and restarted, but the third place I was racing for before encountering Delatang became a ninth at the chequered flag. So, instead of a possible 16 points for third, I scored just seven in the first race of the season - thanks to a gun-shy lapper. Delatang had freaked out when the dice between Noriyuki Haga and me caught up with him. Haga came underneath him going about 30 km/h faster, and the Frenchman just picked his Yamaha up and headed for the grass, taking me with him.

In the second race at the Island, there was another battle with Haga, only this time we disputed the lead. A lot of people don't like racing with Noriyuki, because his bike slides this way and that, but I've always found him a fierce but fair rider. He'll never deliberately run you wide; he always shows some dignity and respect. That's more than I could say for my Honda teammates at times. It was a race long battle that day at Phillip Island, and this time a lapped rider didn't get in the way. I lost the second race by 0.071 of a second, fair and square.

You could say I lost six of those four and half points that Carl Fogarty won the title by at the next round at Donington, Great Britain. I had finished fourth in the first race with Fogarty seventh, but the second was run in two halves. Chris Walker's Kawasaki blew up and they stopped the race. It annoyed me at the time because I noticed Carl had started the warm-up lap with a leaking fuel cap. I was sure Carl would run out of fuel. Ducati team manager Davide Tardozzi was sufficiently concerned they wouldn't have enough fuel to finish the race that he'd taped Carl's fuel cap down. With the restart, Carl was able to refuel. I was covering Fogarty, running in third with two laps to go. All I had to do was finish within one second of Carl to beat him in the combined results. The bike started missing and it coughed and spluttered to the line allowing him to get a gap. My bike stopped completely on the slow-down lap at turn one. Crossing the finish line I left two fist dents in the top of the tank. A wire had broken in the wiring loom.

Then there were the 30 points I lost at the third round at Monza. I lost five of them in the first race by underestimating my new teammate. I had dominated qualifying, won Superpole, so I knew I could pull another second on him anytime I wanted. I lead at first, and then Akira Yanagawa had a huge crash on the Kawasaki. Approaching the crash scene, I could see oil flags everywhere, the Kawasaki in flames. So I braked a little earlier than usual, to let whoever was behind me pass, and it happened to be Colin. I thought, "That's cool, if there's any oil or debris on the track, he'll hit it first". But there was no oil, so he was in the lead, I was second, and our RC45s could not make a gap on the three Ducatis behind us - Chili, Carl and Corser. Every time we tried to put a gap on them, they'd come with us. I was feeling incredibly confident, and felt I could pass Colin anytime I wanted. I felt I had the race in the palm of my hand. So, I decided to let Colin go for a while, and save what was left of my tyres for the final laps. It seemed like a move of pure genius at the time. So I went into cruise control, eased it back a bit to let the Ducatis bunch up. I decided there were enough laps left that I could hold them back for a bit, let the red bikes build up some sort of traffic jam, then pull the pin, leave them behind and catch and pass Colin. Well, the first bit worked, then the second, but the third? I caught him up again, and went to outbrake him into the Parabolica for the last time. That didn't work so I then decided to get the draft and slingshot past him on the way to the flag. When I went to pull out and pass him, I couldn't. He had such a streamlined tuck all the way to the back of the seat, there was no way to draft by him. It was something I noticed about all my Honda teammates. They had more top speed than me because I push more wind. Colin was fastest of them all, but Kocinski was faster, even Carl was faster than me. I blame my riding style on the RC45, which seemed to broaden my shoulders. I had to settle for second at Monza that day, and 20 points instead of 25.

The second race I finally did pass Colin for the lead. But there's an old saying in racing that your bike goes faster when it's about to blow up. That's just what my bike did. As I shifted into top gear on the fastest part of the circuit, crossing the finish line for the penultimate time, the engine dropped a rod and caught on fire. One lap less in practice would have ensured at least another 20 points. I knew something was up as I pulled out of the slipstream of Colin's bike for the first time that weekend. Boom! It let go and I had my answer. So, I left one of my favourite circuits after setting all the fastest laps, with 20 points in the bag, when it could have so easily been 50.

Albacete is another of my favourite tracks; despite the way it favours the extra grunt of the Ducatis off the corners. I was second fastest in the first practice session, and fastest in the first qualifying. But the Superpole was a joke. It started raining with the five fastest guys yet to run, so our times on the wet track were compared with those that had set their time in the dry. I was placed sixth, so I raced off the second row. In the wet, first race I finished fourth, first of the 750s behind three Ducatis - Chili, Corser, and hometrack hero Gregorio Lavilla. In the second, dry race, I finished second to Fogarty, after the quick shifter stopped working.

The German round was held at the Nurburgring that year, the first time the World Superbikes had ever raced there. In unofficial practice on Wednesday for all the teams to learn the circuit, I blew everyone away, with a time that was 1.2 seconds faster than anyone else. In the last qualifying session I was trying to go even faster, as I was now full of confidence and still on pole. I crashed, losing the front into a downhill lefthander. I had to get out the spare bike for the Superpole session and, not being as comfortable on it, I finished sixth and had to start off the second row of the grid again. Next day I woke up to rain again!!! I knew how good the red bikes had been the week before in the wet. I still won the first race. It had taken me until the fifth round to finally win a race in 1998, yet I felt I'd been the fastest rider at each of the rounds so far. I had languished in fifth or sixth place on the points table, when I should have been leading it. The second race at the Nurburgring was another lost opportunity to win the championship. I lost another seven sure points when

I crashed out of second place on the last corner of the track. After doing a somersault for the crowd, I picked my bike up and again the handlebars were intact. I restarted to finish fourth. I wheelied the length of the straight on the last lap to the biggest cheer of the crowd. It had been a heroic ride as bits and pieces were hanging off the bike. Not my trusty new handlebars though. Ducati tried to protest that I had help restarting the bike, but I'd restarted it myself, and the officials overturned their protest.

Although I left Germany in only fourth place in the championship, Ducati could see from my form in the official practice sessions that I was the man to beat in 1998. It wasn't the early championship leader Haga who was posing the biggest threat to their title hopes. Honda had rattled Ducati to the core by winning the title in 1997, and they were dead scared it would happen again in 1998. That's why they made sure Troy Corser came back to World Superbike that year. Fogarty had let them down in 1997 and, the way he went at the start of 1998, especially in the wet, they must have been glad they'd persuaded Troy to come back.

At Misano, Ducati's worst nightmare came true. I won both races at a track where I'd finished 13th and 16th in 1995 - the year Honda had first switched the RC45 onto the Michelins. They were two of the most masterful races I ever rode. In the first I didn't make a good start, but caught up to leader Corser about the middle of the race. I was sitting behind him going "This is good, this is very, very good", because I knew I had plenty in reserve. So, I decided to pass and see if I could make a break on him. Troy must have thought I'd chosen a softer rear Michelin and he let me go thinking the tyre would go off and he would easily pick me off. He actually fell back to third at one stage, before coming back very strongly in the closing laps. But he never caught up. In the second race, I knew he would come back even stronger, because he would have sussed out the tyre situation between the races. The Michelin people attached to the Ducati team would have told him "Aaron's using this..."

In the second race, I was sitting behind Corser again, and my pit board indicated Carl was on the charge behind me. So, I sat there, as cool as can be, thinking, "As soon as Carl gets within one second of us, I'm outta here, I'm gone". One Ducati rider is easier to pass than two, and if I'd waited until Carl caught us, it could have got messy. So, I watched the board, watching the margin reduce. On the very lap the board said "+0.9", I let it rip. I passed Troy at the exact same point I had passed everyone that weekend. I used a much tighter line entering the left-hander onto the back straight and could carry the corner speed out to stay in front. I just went flat out for the last 12 laps. I couldn't have gone any faster, and Troy couldn't have gone any faster, and that's the way it finished. Ducati had made Misano their own track for years. It was the place they tested at most often. It felt absolutely awesome as a four-cylinder rider to beat them there. I couldn't think of a better place to score my first double win. The Misano haul of 50 points vaulted me from fourth place in the championship to second, just six points behind leader Corser.

The luck didn't last for long. At the next round at Kylami in South Africa, I made the mistake of trying to use smaller brake discs to help the bike change direction more easily. It was the wrong move, and the brakes quickly glazed up in the first race, extending my braking points and forcing me back to eighth. In the second race I went back to my normal 320mm discs, and I chased Lavilla through the tricky section of the track called the Bomb Hole on the first lap. Suddenly his Ducati lost all its coolant and he crashed in front of me. Those who went around the outside of his leaky Ducati got away with it. Those who tried to tighten their line and sneak through the inside of the red bike didn't. Jamie Whitham on the Suzuki, and I were a couple of the unlucky ones. I picked the RC45 up again (this was becoming a habit during the 1998 season; thank God I had pushed the handlebar debate), and finished eighth. Colin finished fourth, and I'm sure if it hadn't been for Lavilla's bike lubricating the track, I would have beaten him. South Africa was another round where the "if only..." could apply. Yet despite the incident I came away from South Africa with a one-point lead in the championship, because Troy had an even worse day.

At least the Lavilla incident left me in relatively good shape, unlike what happened in the following round at Laguna Seca, California. It's no secret that I hate Laguna. The pit facilities are atrocious - you end up working out of containers and tents while watching your back - and the racetrack is downright dangerous. There's little run-off before you hit a concrete wall at Laguna, and it doesn't help when the officials make it even more dangerous. I had got fifth in Superpole, and had got a reasonably good start in the first race, when it was stopped because of Yanagawa's dramatic crash at the Corkscrew. Doug Chandler had caused the accident when one of his Muzzy constructed handlebars had broken off in his hand. He couldn't restart, so the officials left his place on the grid empty, instead of moving everyone, who had qualified behind him, up a grid position. So, everyone in the rows behind aimed for this gap in the traffic as the flag fell. It caused a huge crash on the start line. Aaron

Yates, riding for Suzuki America, hooked my handlebar after he came through the gap. It made my bike exit stage right, and I was smacked by another bike, and went down. I slid along the front straight, the bike on top of me, and another three people running over me. I got up and hobbled over to the concrete wall. There was carnage all over the grid - battered bikes and bodies everywhere. I had a dislocated knee, and a cut in my foot that required 15 stitches. As I sat on the wall, it looked like a bomb has gone off. There were riders down, bikes and debris all over the place. There would be no more racing for me that day. My points lead evaporated as I watched Troy finish second in the second race after I returned to the track from the medical centre. He'd been credited with the first race win after the officials decided not to restart the race a third time.

Nor would there be a Suzuka 8-Hour for me in 1998. Honda were still keen for me to race, but after Laguna I couldn't walk, let alone ride. After Laguna, I flew back to New Zealand to recuperate, and Honda phoned to see if I would be riding in the 8-Hour. I said I needed the full three weeks between the Laguna and Brand Hatch rounds to mend for the championship chase. I asked Honda, "Why don't you get John Kocinski to ride?" They said he couldn't ride because he was having an operation on his finger. I had seen John at Laguna and he had a Band-aid on his pinkie. I don't know how John got away with all the things he did with Honda.

Three weeks later, I was still stiff and sore as we lined up on the Brands Hatch grid. In the first race I followed Colin to the chequered flag. My knee was just too stiff to mount any real challenge to him. I felt I needed pain killing injections but was nervous about losing the feeling in my foot. The Honda 1-2 had not gone unnoticed in the Ducati camp. They quickly extracted our tyre info from Michelin, and smoked us once they started using the same tyres. Corser won, followed by Fogarty, then Whitham on the Suzuki. Colin was fourth, and I was fifth. I had now dropped 30 points behind Corser. If only I had the luxury of the team orders I had obeyed in my Kawasaki days. There were five points right there in that first race as I was a wheel length away from winning.

There was another three-week break before round 10 at the A1 ring in Austria. I pushed the team for a test to overcome the brake problems during this time. I trained hard back in Monaco, getting my leg into shape and, in the week before going to Austria, we tested the bike at Brno in Czechoslovakia. It was there that Norris and I hit on the solution to our brake problems, by sneaking the Nissin master cylinder into the system. The A1 ring is hard on brakes, so we were desperate to find something that worked, something that could be relied on all race long. I knew I could only win in Austria on the brakes, and everything went exactly as I planned it. I dominated every practice session, and won the Superpole. In the races, the Ducatis were pulling bike lengths out of me coming off the corners. The only place I passed anybody all weekend was on the brakes. The second corner at the A1 ring is a tight right-hander with a minimum speed of about 30km/h. I remember I was leading Carl through it one time and, as soon as he opened the gas, he came right past me, staring right at me with those bug eyes. I remember thinking, "You bastard, if only I had your engine". He got up to a second and a half in front, but I wasn't going to let him go. I just out-rode him in the final laps, and he got so demoralised he let Chili get by him for second. In the second race, I dished out the same medicine. I just hunted

Carl down, and then broke him like he was made of clay. The double victory closed the gap to Troy to just 1.5 points. Colin, using the full Brembo brake system, finished seventh and ninth that day.

At Assen, I wanted to beat Carl again. He always went so well there, I wanted to do another Misano - beat Fogarty and the Ducati at a track where they'd been dominant for years. It went to plan in the first day. I set the fastest time. Then the fickle Dutch weather came into play. It rained the second day, so I was fastest qualifier going into the Superpole. I had crashed my number one bike in the wet second practice session on Saturday and had to use number two for the Superpole. They had rectified the problems with Superpole and were now using the F1 rules in wet conditions - a twelve lap maximum. I ended up in grid position number eight. For the first race I chose the hard construction rear tyre that had worked for my practice fastest lap. It proved to be the wrong choice. There just hadn't been enough dry practice to sort out tyres for race day, and I rode my butt off to finish fourth behind three Ducati riders headed for the podium - Chili, Fogarty and Corser. In the second race I quickly switched to a softer construction rear tyre, and the bike hooked up a lot better. I finished second to Carl, after he and Chili had the infamous coming together on the last lap which ensured Chili would never again ride a Ducati after that season.

With one round to go Corser led me in the points by a scant 0.5 of a point. He had 328.5 points to my 328. There was nearly a month between Assen and the final round at Sugo in Japan, and we put everything into preparing for those final two races. I trained like never before, while Honda developed new engine and brake parts for Colin and me to test. If only Michelin had been doing their homework as well...

The tyres wouldn't work all weekend, and the traction problems were worse for the 750cc 4's, because of engine characteristics that favoured horsepower rather than torque. In the first practice session I was first, then in first qualifying I struggled to eighth fastest time. Things improved a bit for the second qualifying and I moved up to third fastest. Then during Superpole I slipped to 10th. Tenth on the grid in the most important race of the year, and possibly my life!

I tried so damn hard to be fast all weekend, but knew in the back of my mind the tyres would not hang on for race distance. There was some brilliance in the qualifying lap times, but it was false hope. At this stage, I was only hopeful of overhauling Troy rather than my usual confident self. I knew his red bike would be a lot more user friendly to the Michelins.

But where was Troy - the guy I'd been chasing all year? He crashed in warm-up that morning, and ruptured his spleen. He was out for the rest of the year. We waited for him to show up on the grid for the first race of the day at Sugo, and when he didn't, I went up to Carl and said to him, "This is between you and me now". He was five and a half points behind me in the championship. On the way back to my bike, I saw Neil Hodgson had his race face on. He had finally qualified well and was trying to secure a decent job for the coming season so had some points to prove that day. I went up to the Kawasaki rider and said: "If I stick my wheel up the inside of you, can you give me some room?" I don't know why I said that; maybe I had a premonition of what was about to happen. Anyway, Neil said yes, and I went to my bike.

The flag dropped, and Neil did absolutely everything he could to beat me. He'd run me out to the grass and I had to take avoiding action. I'd come through on the brakes, and he'd tip his bike on top of mine. Or I'd get past, and he'd wait until an impossible time to brake and maintain corner speed, scrub it all off to make the turn, and hold me up again. It went on all race long, and the more it went on, the madder I got. I ended up using up all my tyres trying to get around him, and finished seventh just behind him.

On the slow down lap, I was fuming. As I went by Neil I used my free hand to punch him in the kidneys. He wagged his finger at me, going "naughty-naughty". I thought, "Right, let's sort this out here and now", and pulled over to the side of the track, resting my bike on the fence. Neil stopped as well and was sitting on his bike mouthing off at me. So, I went up, grabbed the chin piece of his helmet, and dragged him off his bike. I was so angry this clown had just ruined my lead in the championship. Especially as I thought we'd agreed that if he saw my wheel, he wouldn't carve me up. The TV cameras caught up with us at the end of the incident.

Carl finished third that first race, and now held a 1.5-point advantage going into the second race. I was fired up, and rocketed from 10th on the grid to fourth place by the first corner. Carl was third. He then started pulling half a second out of me every lap. We just didn't have a rear tyre capable of winning a championship that day. The Honda was just spinning up out of every corner, leaving dark lines of rubber everywhere, but it just wouldn't drive forward. I gave it everything mentally and physically that day, yet I finished sixth. Carl finished fourth, and he won the championship by 4.5 points, with a total of 351.5 to 347.

One month later, I was back at Sugo for a one-off international race called the TBC, named after a television company. It was a rare opportunity to race Mick Doohan on equal terms. He rode my spare

RC45, brought out his mechanics from the Grand Prix, and also had half of my mechanics to help them get up to speed with a four stroke. With him came a Michelin technician who threw in a few tyres he thought might work on the Superbike. They worked so much better than the tyres we had tried at the World Superbike round four weeks earlier. It was another "if only..." to conclude 1998.

I qualified fastest for the TBC race, and it was a time faster than any recorded during practice for the World Superbikes. In the race I won the holeshot to the first corner, and led for the first 10 laps. Then Tady Okada caught up, and we had a bit of a scrap for the second half of the race. It was all decided in the last chicane. I tried to go up the inside of Okada, but found a lapped rider in my way. The chance was gone so I put all my effort into getting a good drive off the chicane to beat him to the line. We crossed the line side by side, Tady winning by 0.05 of a second, and Mick finished 2.5 seconds behind me in third, with Colin another 2.5 seconds behind him. I knew the pace up front had been good, so I compared the total race time, because it was the same distance as the Superbike races held four weeks earlier. It was 10 seconds faster than the fastest race at Sugo the month before. And it was all because of the tyre difference. We were riding the same bikes; they hadn't changed at all. All that changed was a Michelin tyre engineer from the Grand Prix scene, with some tyres he thought might work on a superbike. "Where were you a month ago?" I asked him.

Later, Carl told me that Mick Doohan had said to him that, "You know, if Aaron had raced as hard during the World Superbike Season as he did at the TBC race, he could have been world champion." I couldn't believe my ears. This was just hearsay from Carl, so I wasn't sure whether Mick ever said it or not. Even so, my passing thoughts were "Mate, you don't know the half of it."

ten

Basic Instincts and Head Games

It had been hard to gather any enthusiasm for the TBC race after the disappointment of losing the championship. I felt totally drained. I put my lethargic mood down to the depression that comes with losing. Little did I know at the time that it was caused by something a lot more serious and sinister. I remember telling Eurosport commentator Jonathan Green, in a TV interview after the last race of the 1998 championship, that I just felt like going home and sleeping for a month. When the call came to race Mick in Japan, my first reaction was "What for?" It wasn't like me at all. Normally I'd jump at a chance to show the HRC bosses that I deserved a 500 ride as much as the multi-world champ. This was one of the only opportunities I had been given to race Mick on the same machine. I should have been jumping out of my skin to show what I was made of. But I just wanted to stay home and rest.

In the week following the TBC race, I stayed in Japan to test the VTR V-twin prototype. I rode the VTR V-twin during these sessions, as HRC wanted me to personally assess its potential before proceeding any further with it. It was a blast. It wasn't as fast in top-end power as the RC45 V4; it was actually 15-20 km hour slower down the long back straight of Suzuka, but it had a heap more torque, with a Ducati-like lunge off the corners. When I got a great tow from Shinichi Itoh on the RC45, I recorded a lap of 2:09.71 around Suzuka. This was as fast as Colin on his RC45, and it sealed the decision to develop the V-twin further, and race it in the 2000 season. If this test had not gone well, and I hadn't been positive about the VTR, then HRC would have reassessed its viability as a race bike. The bike was at a raw stage of development, and needed to undergo a lot of changes before the 2000 season. It was very slow down the straights.

While I was at HRC, I organised a meeting to talk about the problems we had experienced in 1998, particularly those involving the brakes. It was in this meeting that the question was asked, "Why did you lose the championship?" So, I started talking about the brakes, and how we had only a couple of trouble-free rounds without brake dramas. Then one guy suddenly interrupted me, "Well, if you didn't crash at the Nurburgring, we would have won". I was stunned by the comment. I felt like walking out right then and there. I felt like saying, "If the fucking bike didn't drop a rod at Monza, we would have won". And "If Michelin had bought the right tyres to Sugo, we would have won". If HRC had let us use the Nissin master cylinder we would have won. If the wiring harness didn't break at Donington we would have won. If the quick shifter didn't stop working at Albacete we would have won. No one could pinpoint where we lost the championship, because something went wrong every bloody weekend. When the problems were overcome I would win - Nurburgring, Misano, and the A1 Ring were proof. Besides, that character had forgotten the aftermath of the crash at Nurburgring. I picked my bike up and finished fourth. Most of the damage done to the bike that day was to the fairing, which just hung on as I crossed the finish line on the back wheel. The crowd went berserk. I could hear them cheering me on above the noise of the bike. At least they appreciated my efforts.

The brake problem wasn't just a problem for me, despite whispers among some of the media covering the paddock that it was related to my right hand disabilities. If that was so, how come all the riders were having the same brake binding problem. One of the most noticeable incidents was the time Lavilla was starting his Superpole lap at Donington. As he wheelied off the last corner to start his fast lap the front wheel had locked. When it came down he left a five metre black mark with the front tyre and proceeded to retire into the pits. It had dogged superbikes ever since the FIM took away carbon composite disc brakes. The justification was to make superbikes more comparable to the road bikes on which they are based. But there's little correlation between a road RC45 and my factory racer and, by banning the composite discs in 1995, the FIM increased the dangers of racing. For 1999, we had to find a solution to the brake-dragging problem. It really came to a head when Colin crashed while testing and damaged his shoulder. Desperate measures were needed. The Brembo system was replaced with Nissin brakes, but that did not completely solve the problem either.

It was getting hard to test anything. I was just feeling so shite. Between the TBC race, the HRC meeting, and our first tests before the 1999 season, I had done a lot of publicity engagements - flown here, flown there, and it was all catching up to me. Our first test in '99 was Kyalami, and it went pretty well. Then we flew straight to Phillip Island; I had the speed, but no stamina. The surface had just been resealed, and I broke the lap record three laps into the test. Broke it by a second because of the new seal. No one else was going as fast as me. Then I went out again and went faster, then crashed. I started wondering what was going on. I just didn't have my usual feel for traction, and the crash happened without me even knowing. I just wasn't as sharp as usual.

The next test day I did only 25 laps. I fell asleep in the pit, and just couldn't be bothered. It was a total contrast to my usual attitude. Before, if we had a five-day test, I would be out the whole time from nine until five clocking up the laps. Here I was sleeping in the middle of the test day as I couldn't concentrate and needed to rest my mind.

These were important test sessions, because we were not only getting the RC45 ready for the 1999 season, but there was the VTR to test as well. I was feeling so bad I said to HRC I didn't want to test the twin if I wasn't going to race it that season. I didn't want to lose focus on the bike we were about to race and I also thought the extra work would just wear me out. They then tempted me with the opportunity of a one-day test on the NSR500 GP bike, and a compromise was reached. I would test their V-twin, and they would give me a couple of hours on the NSR. I arrived at the Phillip Island test, had dinner, went to bed, and woke up at about 2 a.m. in the morning with some gastro bug. For the rest of the night, I sat on the toilet, covering that end, while throwing up in the bath at the same time. Next day, I went to the hospital and got them to put me on a glucose drip to rehydrate. I finally made it to the track around 2 p.m. I then asked

HRC if it was OK to test the next day. They said, "Today is your day and we don't want you going out on the NSR in your condition right now".

Their excuse was there was too much work on the VTR to do, and they couldn't afford to sacrifice another hour of track time to the NSR and me. Ironically, the next week, at the test at Eastern Creek, we would run out of engines for the VTR and go home early. After all I had done for them. I thought, "Thanks for nothing". Colin however, did get to ride the NSR on the last day at Phillip Island. He looked really good on it, lapping within a second of Mick's times. This confirmed to me, as I'd been faster than Colin through most of the testing, that I could have done as good a job or better on the two-stroke, if only I had been given the chance.

We moved from Phillip Island to Eastern Creek, but the weather was bad, and the test was called off after Colin cold seized a couple of engines. They had more work to do on the V-twin motor before testing could resume. I felt relieved, because it would mean a few more days rest before heading to Laguna Seca to resume testing the RC45. We went to Laguna Seca for a two-day test, where Colin damaged his shoulder after the brakes dragged on at the infamous Corkscrew. Our fuel hadn't arrived, so again our test was cut short, and I had to try to test everything necessary within the distance our fuel allotment would allow - about 40 laps at the most. This test was to make the final choice of different parts to be used on the RC45 for the 1999 season. HRC needed confirmation. It was hard to make informed choices on the parts with so little opportunity to test each one, but I had to do it all after Colin's crash.

When we arrived at Kylami, South Africa for the first round of the 1999 season, I couldn't stop yawning. I was so tired. I swam in the mornings to get me good and alert for the job, but I was feeling really clapped out. In the races I got a second and third. Carl Fogarty just cleared off in the distance, and he beat me by 10 seconds in the first race, and seven in the second. I remember thinking, "Something's wrong, he's not that good a rider to beat me by such a margin".

Between South Africa and the second round at Phillip Island, HRC rang up to arrange a test in Japan. I asked what they wanted to test, and they said "brake pads". The test was the Monday and Tuesday in Japan of the race week of Phillip Island, Australia. It would mean flying all Wednesday to start the race weekend Friday morning. I just wasn't up for that. I didn't see the brake pads as the problem. My impression was there was something wrong with the braking system. The pads would not solve that. But again, I was making decisions around my need for rest, automatically without even being conscious of doing so. Colin and Adrian went and, all weekend at Phillip Island, Adrian told me how "great" the test was. It was the first test session I ever missed in my life, and I should've known right there and then there was something seriously wrong with me.

While my edge was sliding away, Colin was becoming more and more aggressive. I noticed his new attitude in the pit. If there was a test session where I was faster than him, he'd keep on trying and trying to better my time. With Adrian firing him up, it was as if he had to always be the fastest Honda rider out there. I remember saying to Megan, "There's something different about Colin this year". We'd got quite close to Colin and his girlfriend Alyssia, from when they first came to Europe in 1995. We'd drive our motorhomes to races in convoy, and generally helped them settle into the World Superbike scene. Sometimes in the off-season, we visited them back in North America, and the four of us went on a skiing trip together to Colorado. I knew when Colin joined Castrol Honda that our friendship might not survive the rivalry that exists between teammates. It ended at the third round of the 1999 championship, one and three quarter laps into the second race of the day at Donington Park, when Colin succeeded in doing what John Kocinski failed to do at Sentul in 1997. He sent me tumbling from my bike after running into me. The whole incident could have been so easily avoided.

I was already feeling tired and emotional from the first race. I had chucked everything at Carl Fogarty, extracted every ounce of energy from the bike and my body. Yet I couldn't get the gap down to less than 2.5 seconds. Carl saw me coming from his pit board, yet he controlled my charge from the front. When I did a fast lap, he did a fast lap, and he just kept the gap at 2.5 seconds. It had taken everything from me, and I remember blurting out on TV after the race that I was sick of being "Carl Fogarty's whipping boy".

Part way through the second lap of the second race, it looked like Carl would pull a gap on the rest of the field again. He was second, with teammate Troy Corser towing him along. I was thinking, "If I don't pick up a place at every braking point, then this race is lost". Between the Ducatis and me there was Chili on the Suzuki, and Colin. As we entered the Melbourne Loop, Colin went to out-brake Chili, just as I decided to out-brake Colin. So I decided the safest manoeuvre was to let the brakes off a bit more and pass them both, knowing it would cost me time in the apex of the corner and that somebody might pass me on the way out. It was the safest thing to do at the time as Colin had now come over onto my line. I turned the bike and was on the gas coming out. Colin had a better line, and was on the gas earlier and was now beside me. He then let his bike run wide knowing I was on the outside of him. He could have easily taken a slightly tighter exit. I backed off, desperate to make some room. My handlebar got caught on his knee, then his seat piece just as the front wheel run out of tarmac. Down I went, the bike trapping my hand on the ripple strip. I immediately jumped up and gave Colin the finger, because he was looking back to survey the damage.

I picked the bike up again, and restarted, but there was something wrong with my throttle hand. The bike wasn't too flash either, and I pulled straight into the pits to get the fairing replaced. My crew were a bit reluctant, but I yelled at them - "Just fix the fucking thing, will ya." I got back out just in front of Colin, who was now leading the race. I eased back to let him lap me, just so I could tell him how I felt again. When he came past, I stared straight at him, and flipped him off again, putting my hand right in front of his face. Then I tucked in behind him, as my conscience told me it was the right thing to do. I followed him for around five laps. I thought if I remained behind Colin it would make it harder for Carl to catch and pass. About five laps went by and my now newly broken and mangled finger was starting to make my hand go numb. There's a corner at Donington where you brake, then let off the brake a little for some bumps. Maybe I held onto the brake for too long, and locked up the front wheel on the bumps. When I jumped up from the crash, my finger was just hanging there.

People think I hurt my hand in that second crash, but it was definitely the first. There was blood all over the handlebars and the side of the bike from the laps I raced between the two crashes. The marshals told me I had to stay there until the end of the race, but I told them I was about to lose my finger, and crossed the track and some guy gave me a lift on the back of his bike. I went straight to the medical centre, where the doctors said if I wanted to stay in the championship and ride in a couple of weeks time it would be easier to take the finger off. No thanks, sunshine! I had become attached to my little finger since Dr Glasson had saved it in 1990, plus I like to cut all my fingernails. So, I talked with Neil and he organised a visit to his specialist in Wales the next day, a Dr Witek Mintowt-Czyz.

That night Colin came to see me in my motorhome. He appeared at the door, smiling. He said, "Did you see that as a racing incident?" By this time, I had replayed the incident on video over and over again, and was facing the prospect of losing my finger. I said, "That's not what happened, you deliberately ran me off the racetrack." It really pissed me off that he just went straight into how he felt it was a racing incident. There was no concern about the finger; he just wanted to offload his guilt by trying to convince himself it was a racing incident. Megan's father, John, was there, and he ushered Colin outside before things turned ugly, saying there was nothing more to talk about.

Every time I talked to Neil about what happened, he claimed not to have watched the incident on video. He wouldn't make a call, wouldn't censure Colin for what he had done. He chose to ignore it, hoping it would go away. In the next few days, faced with the finger damage, I felt there was little or no support from Neil over the incident. So, everything got out of hand within the team. It was "us"and "them" within our pit. The media got wind of it, and the headlines read "Castrol Honda at War," and they weren't far from the truth. With stronger management, we could have sorted it out in a week or two. Instead, the bitterness brewed away for months, reducing our competitiveness, and helping Carl Fogarty to a title he didn't have to work hard for.

The next race meeting was Albacete, 10 days later. It was always going to be a struggle to ride the bike let alone drive the motorhome. I had heard little or nothing from team management in that time. However, Norris came to the rescue and flew to Monaco, and drove me in the motorhome to Spain.

I had struggled to drive the motorhome all the way back to Monaco after seeing Witek, the surgeon, in Wales. In Spain, I took off the finger brace and rode. I didn't take any pain killing injections as I thought the risk of the hand going numb was too great. I had to get an oversize glove stretched so that it would fit over my finger, as it was twice the usual size, and it was very hard to grip the bar. The injury was complicated by the fact that I had plates and screws in there already from the 1990 rebuild. I was not doing it any favours by riding in Albacete and knew that the bones would be struggling to knit accurately. After the weekend the finger felt all mushy again like it had been re-broken. It did in fact mend over the next six weeks, but needed corrective surgery in the off-season, again performed by Dr Glasson.

During the races, I finished a credible fourth and seventh. But the finger was very bad. Every time I turned the bike, gripped the bars to stop the thing from wobbling, or went for the brake, I'd feel my glove fill with more ooze. I didn't remove the glove between races, as it was too much of an effort to get it back on. It murdered my lap times, as it was hard to be smooth with the throttle and the brakes at this stop and go track.

To make matters worse, a TV crew followed me around for a couple of weeks. They were making a programme for the new millennium called "Coming Home", about successful New Zealanders living and working overseas. The show was to profile a wide range of talents, from the arts, theatre, sports, TV and movies. If only it had been any other year. They caught one of the lowest points of the season when I was black-flagged at Monza, and chucked out of the race. They did manage to make a great show, despite all the drama at one of my favourite tracks, but it would have been nice if they'd been able to capture one of my wins there instead of a fiasco. The start lights had gone out, but there was a delay before they turned green, and several riders were called in for a stop-and-go penalty for jumping the start. The officials didn't notify my pit crew to bring me in for a stop-and-go within the next three laps. Instead, they put a black flag out at the start line (Monza has two separate start and finish lines) and below this was a board with my number 111 on it. This was Monza, where you go down the front straight at 320 km/h, and I didn't notice the flag in time. When I finally pulled in, I was chucked out of the race. It made me wild that the officials didn't notify my pit and get them to signal on my board as this was the only thing that I took my eyes off the racetrack for. Monza has one of the fastest straights of the year and when you are busy slipstreaming four other guys and watching the rev counter to change gear at the perfect spot, you are not looking at what's going on anywhere else.

There was more going wrong with me than black flags and broken fingers however. I had not been feeling myself and decided to go to the circuit doctors and see if they could arrange for some blood tests. So I ended up going to the Rimini hospital while at Misano the following week. I got the results back and asked the Italian doctors to go over them for me. The tests they ran were all negative. I was higher than normal in creatine levels but this was not uncommon for an athlete.

Fogarty's main rival for the title in 1999 was his teammate Corser, and the red brigade won 16 World Superbike races that year, helped by engine changes that made the 996 easier to ride. Meanwhile Carl was regressing the bike back to his favourite 1995 Ducati. He ripped out the front end - a fantastic pair of 46 mm Ohlins forks - and replaced them with 42 mm versions, saying this improved front tyre feedback. It wasn't the sort of change I'd endorse; I would have tuned the stiffer front end until it provided the level of feedback I wanted, but Carl is Carl, and his results in 1999 made it hard to say he was doing anything wrong.

Fogarty won the title with a record points tally of 489. Corser and Edwards finished with 361 each, the runner-up position going to Colin on account of his two extra race wins 5-3. I finished fourth on 323, mainly as a result of seven second place positions and more times on the podium than in 1998. I didn't win one race that whole miserable year. I came closest to winning at Hockenheim and the Nurburgring - when Carl chucked the Ducati away in front of me, at the end of the downhill straight. The rules regarding fall down sensors were changed for 1999. Previously the bike sensor would stop the engine as soon as the bike was horizontal. This was a safety feature to protect the rider and the marshals.

Basic Instincts and Head Games

Ducati instigated a rule change, which meant the bikes were allowed to remain ticking over for at least 10 seconds on their side. Ducati were frustrated with the ease I managed to restart my bike after crashing the year before. There is no way you can restart a Ducati. But if it is still running on the ground, it is easy enough to pull the clutch in and get going. This is what made it possible for Carl to continue. I should have won, but the tyres went off and the brakes were dragging, which was making me push the front. Corser went on a charge, breaking the lap record for the last three laps, and ended up lunging past me at the final chicane as I was now struggling under brakes. He won by 0.2 of a second.

At Hockenheim I won the first race, even received the chequered flag, only to have the victory overturned. Everyone knows that, at Hockenheim, you don't want to be leading on the last lap because you'll tow whoever's second to the win. I played my cards to perfection that day. Carl Fogarty led going into the last lap of the race, and I passed him in the stadium section just before the flag. The first five guys actually received the chequered flag. Then from sixth place on they received a red flag.

The officials displayed it because Peter Goddard had a tyre fly apart at 295km/ hour and Igor Jerman rammed into him, causing a horrific crash behind us. They should never display a red flag on the last lap as next time past the incident everyone will be at crawling speed anyway - race over! We five guys at the front had already finished the race and received the chequered flag before the incident occurred, as we were nearly one lap in front. However, the red flag rule they applied now saw the race being taken back a lap and me placed second. I was fuming, as I and four others hadn't received a red flag until our race was over. It was only on the warm down lap that we came across the incident and red flags. Carl verbally agreed that I had won the race fair and square even though the revised result gave him enough points to take the title. I was totally shattered. It was like, "What do I have to do to win a race this year?" As I approached the podium, I thought "There's no way I'm going to stand on the second spot on the rostrum." I asked Neil what he thought about a podium boycott, and he just said, "That's up to you". So I spun on my heels and headed back to my pit. The organisers slapped a 500 Swiss franc fine on me for my trouble.

Before the last round at Sugo, I spoke to Barry Sheene about Chronic Fatigue Syndrome. All the symptoms were similar to what I was experiencing, so I thought why not? He advised me to have a 20-minute cold bath each morning. At the final round at Sugo, that's what I did on race day morning - soaked myself to the core in freezing cold water. It didn't make any difference, and the last races of the RC45 in World Superbike are not the fondest of memories. I finished 16th in the first race, and 13th in the second, just beating Troy Corser. This gave Colin the runner-up position in the world title, and I was tempted to slow down, and let Troy past so he would have got the points to finish second, but that wouldn't have been fair to the team, despite what happened at Donington.

After six seasons, the RC45 was being put out to pasture. To me it was the most technically developed bike of the 1990s World Superbike era, and it was just the rules that stopped it winning more races. It was a mechanical genius compared to Ducati's 'work of art' - the 916. I had been asking Honda throughout my career if I could get to keep one as I felt it was my baby. I had been with it from its birth and it had now developed, with my input, into an awesome beast. The answer was always, "When you win the world championship". This was the carrot they always dangled, which would brass me off, as I knew most of my racebikes ended up in the crusher. When it was confirmed we would race the VTR, I purchased one of the last RC45s from Honda UK. I've kept it in its box as, to me, it's a collector's item. It was a masterpiece of engineering, the Honda V4, and easily the best 750cc four of its time.

Colin and I stayed in Japan after Sugo to start testing the VTR1000 SP1 for the following Superbike season. We'd go to bed at the same time, but I'd struggle to get up in the morning. It was like my body wanted to sleep 14 hours a day. After testing, I flew back to New Zealand, and starting seeing doctors who talked my language. We took all sorts of samples for analysis, even stool samples, but still no one could say what was wrong with me. I went to a cardio specialist and spent 22 minutes on his treadmill. My heartbeat only reached 173, which he said showed how fit I was. However, I did discover I had a heart murmur, which was a worry for about one day. They then told me that it was common in athletes who have a slow resting pulse. There were nutritionists advising me on special diets, and eye specialists to whom I complained to about my vision - which had lost its sharpness.

While out in New Zealand I drove a Holden V8 in a 500 km endurance race with a mate - Greg Brinck - who had been a New Zealand motocross champion at about the same time I started racing as a junior. We had the race shot to bits, and I was driving down the long back straight of the Pukekohe circuit with a 45 second lead on the next team. We were getting big exposure on the live TV broadcast of the race, when the driveshaft fell off. I thought, "What else can go wrong now?"

I didn't have to wait long. When we went to test the VTR at Phillip Island in February 2000, I went boogie boarding with some of the mechanics. I caught three or four waves, and then I got this huge headache, like someone had stuck a meat cleaver into the side of my skull. I was looking into the sun, its reflection on the water, and it was just like it was killing me with its rays. The glare seemed to be producing this stabbing pain inside my head. Little did I know at the time that I'd had a stroke in the surf that day. For the last year or so, the defective vein I had been born with was weakening and bulging, putting pressure on my brain. It was somewhere down in the brain stem, where it started affecting my vision and causing me fatigue.

The following week we were due to test the VTR at Eastern Creek, but I left the team at the track and went driving that sunny Valentine's Day towards an eventual meeting with Professor Michael Morgan, and a date with his operating table and scalpel. He would cut the side of my head open, and surgically remove a 2cm bleed.

The biggest challenge of my life was about to begin.

eleven

Back From The Dead

Coming around after the operation I felt trapped. I tried to convince Megan and the nurse looking after me that I could be untied and I wouldn't pull out the necessary lines attached to me, or the bandages covering my head. I tried, in a most delirious way, to tell them they could trust me! They took some convincing, as apparently I hadn't been the easiest patient. My return to intensive care from the theatre had seen me irrationally trying to remove anything attached to me. I had become a serious threat to myself. I was also inconsolable and wouldn't be calmed down. It ended with my hands being tied down to the bed to protect myself and it took several people to manage this task. I don't remember any of this.

The nurses had asked Megan to come into intensive care to try to help calm me down. It shocked her to see me thrashing and banging around obviously in pain, tied to the bed. She thought I'd be quietly sedated. She immediately questioned the staff about it and they explained that a level of awareness was required so my vital signs could be read. Not totally convinced, and seeing and hearing me thrashing and moaning in pain, pressured her into asking them to please administer more morphine. They assured her I'd had more than enough, and they couldn't understand why I wasn't settling. As Megan talked more to them, and she explained that I have a very high tolerance to pain, they realised what was happening. The nurse explained that people who use all their mental strength to overcome pain find it difficult to relax and let the drugs take care of their pain. They end up fighting both the pain and the drugs. It made sense as I had always pushed all pain barriers aside and had plenty of experience at it. I was a master of pain denial.

I was talking at this stage but I can't recall anything I said. Megan told me later the catheter attached to my dick was my biggest complaint. I kept thinking I was going to wet the bed. So many liquids are pumped into you after brain surgery that you just need to have a piss, constantly. I was told again and again that it was OK, I had a catheter in place, and it would be fine to relieve myself. It just didn't seem right. I wanted to stand at the urinal and pee like a man should. I was still not absorbing my surroundings at all and couldn't understand what was being said to me. This conversation went on for at least an hour or so.

Slowly I was calmed down, and when I was trusted enough not to cause any more problems the nurses untied my hands. All I wanted to do now was scratch my nose, not rip out the catheter. It was at this point that I became conscious.

I was alive. The operation had obviously been a success. I could think, see, move, speak, and feel the pain. I never really doubted I would survive the operation, but the total success of the surgery was immediately apparent and it was a huge relief. For proof, I only had to open my eyes. I was no longer seeing double.

I had spent four and a half hours on the operating table that night. Professor Morgan removed all the damaged brain tissue, without taking away any of the healthy. The lead-up to the operation was full of worry. That morning, my father and sister had arrived. The day dragged on, and my condition deteriorated rapidly. I had tried to put on a brave face, but as the hours passed, I gave in to the fatigue I was now feeling. I needed to sleep in a darkened room, as any light was painful. Conversation ceased and nausea set in. This may have been caused by anxiety. Inside, there had been real fear. What if the knife slipped? What if the anaesthetic wore off prematurely while Professor Morgan was hard at work? What if they struck a major artery and couldn't stem the blood flow? My op was scheduled for 5p.m., but would eventually take place around 9p.m. It was one of the longest days of my life.

My head had been prepared for surgery, shaved, and marked with guide lines for scalpel and saw. Professor Morgan and his team could now enter at the best location to reach the problem area. I felt some relief the part of the brain he would be operating on didn't affect the personality in any way. I would return from surgery the same old me. The risks were to my vision and fine motor skills. Of course, these are essential when racing a motorcycle and it is obvious now why the 1999 season had been such a struggle.

The hospital had wanted payment up front for the surgery and the days in their care that followed. I had to pull a credit card out and pay for something I was struggling to get my head around, let alone process the payment for it. Payment up front just in case you don't make it. Whoever said that the only two constants in life were death and taxes, forgot to include the bills. It was no vote of confidence, but coming around in intensive care, and finally registering my surroundings, the "what ifs" were over, and the road to recovery was beginning.

Prior to being moved back to the ward after 18 hours in intensive care, I was surprised at the lack of pain. My stay in ICU was shorter than the three days expected, but then they didn't know me! The nurses came and asked me if I needed any Panadol, and I said: "Panadol? Don't even bother." They were also checking my mental faculties, asking me what hospital I was at, and whether I could find the end of my nose with my finger. Their favourite question was, "Who is the prime minister of Australia?" At the time the New Zealand government was changing, and I had no idea who the prime minister of my own country was, let alone Australia's. Over the next few days I started to get better. Then they took the bandages off my head, and I got the biggest shock of all.

There was a huge trapdoor-like scar on the side of my head surrounding my ear. My ear seemed to be about an inch lower than before because the swelling was very impressive. This reduced over time and the ear thankfully returned to its rightful place. I had been under the illusion they would drill a small hole in my head, and somehow suck the bad bits of brain out. I wasn't mentally prepared for the fact that they had to cut my head half open to remove the contamination. When there's a bleed on the brain, it evidently fills the brain cavity with mush, and all this has to be removed. The only way is to have good access; so all kinds of saws and instruments had been used on me. Some months later, a Kiwi doctor told me that the surgery had been particularly delicate and few surgeons could perform this with accuracy. They had to move aside the frontal lobe to reach the brain stem. The frontal lobe should never be touched. This doctor also said that he would not have been able to recommend anybody in New Zealand to perform this surgery. Good thing for me, when my condition reached crisis point, that Eastern Creek was in Sydney.

After a couple of days, I checked out of the hospital and into a luxury B&B round the corner to begin my recuperation. It wasn't necessary for me to have any contact with the hospital until the removal of my stitches. All I had to do was monitor my temperature four times a day. If the temperature moved higher than 37.5, I had to return to the Dalcross Hospital immediately as this would have been a sign of infection. The B&B was a nice place with a swimming pool and tennis court, but suddenly I found I couldn't stand to be around people. It was just too much hard work to talk. One day, I just stared at the pool for hours and hours. I had no book, no music, no stimulation at all. I just stared blankly into space. The whole afternoon passed in some kind of mental stupor. It made me wonder: "Has Professor Morgan removed more brain than I realised?" I stopped worrying when it occurred to me that if I was able to ask the question I was probably going to be OK.

A couple of days later, I realised I needed to stimulate my brain, teaching it to begin living again. So I began reading a book my mother had given me that Christmas about climbing Everest. I started to read because I thought I had to give my mind something to focus on, or else my thoughts would just drift all over the place. Yet it was hard to read anything. I struggled through it and the incredible stories of the mental and physical bravery of the climbers became an inspiration.

I was sensitive to everything. Megan wanted to take a picture of my scars, and I was standing on the balcony of the B&B posing for the camera, pointing the side of my head to the sun. It seemed to take forever. I snapped at her to hurry up and take the fucking photo. I just couldn't stand the sun in my eyes anymore.

Life was just as tough for Megan, if not tougher. She had to deal with all the phone calls during this time. Before the operation there'd been a TV crew camped at the gates of the hospital, asking for information and taking pictures of the hospital exterior to send back to New Zealand. The phone kept on ringing. Everyone wanted to know how I was doing, what I was doing, and where I was doing it. She had to handle it all, while dealing with her own concerns about our future. It wasn't as if she was skilled at PR, and could put a positive spin on everything. Was her husband now a completely different person to the guy she married? All the evidence she had seen so far was pointing that way, although gradually, with time, the old Aaron would return.

The part of the brain Professor Morgan had operated on affects the nervous system, and how the brain processes the information sent to it by the senses. I was now hypersensitive to anything and everything. Going for a walk to the shops for the first time, the noise and rush of the busy traffic was hard to absorb. When people talked to me, it was as if I couldn't process the information into any structured form. The bright light of the sun was just too much to bear.

Meanwhile the B&B landlady seemed loopier than I was feeling. She had some issues. On one occasion she refused to let Megan use the telephone to make a collect call to her brother and, late at night, suggested the phone box at the end of the street. She carried the grandiose title of Lady Robinson. Fortunately her husband was a gentleman. He was very supportive and caring throughout our stay, and took some of the sting out of the little notes of complaint his wife tucked under our door.

We kept our location secret, for obvious reasons, but a few close friends found their way to us. Long time friends Mark and Denise Fisso drove hours along the coast road from Sale to visit. Greg Murphy also gave me a flying visit as he was in Sydney on business. These visits were short and sweet, needed and appreciated, but I was not up to spending much time with anyone.

Two weeks after the operation, they took my stitches out. The nurse-from-hell on duty that day seemed to want to punish me. The pain was incredible and the trauma left my T-shirt wet with sweat. She suggested I should toughen up, so I suggested she should go back to nursing school as I'd probably had more stitches than she'd ever removed. The day before this I took my first drive in a car. Megan and I went to a BBQ at Rob and Carol's, who had also invited Peter and Diana Doyle. This was the first time I had left the B&B for more than lunch. Carol, Diana and Megan hit the champagne, as it was a relief for me to have come this far and something to celebrate. One thing led to another and it was decided it was better if Megan didn't drive. Rob offered to be our chauffeur, but I saw this as an opportunity to get behind the wheel.

Four days later we saw Professor Morgan for the first time since the surgery. He asked a lot of questions and based his prognosis on my answers. He explained every brain is different, and every person different, so the aftercare and the recovery from surgery is never the same. Professor Morgan told me, "Just get on with things. Your brain will let you know if you have overdone it. Fatigue will set in, and that will be your guideline for what you can and can't achieve. Sleep is the most important healer - listen to your body. Avoid alcohol and keep hydrated, but do not overhydrate. Based on this you can do anything, push yourself as hard as you like. There are no risks."

Professor Morgan knew my profession, and thought about my future prior to the surgery. He had opted to screw, plate and glue my skull back into place. Normal procedure would be to just glue and let the bone heal naturally. He knew that I would need a strong skull as soon as possible to begin the rigours of racing. The plates and screws offered me the strength faster than the healing time of a glued together skull.

I had been lucky enough not to have any seizures prior to the stroke, which can be common signs of pressure on the brain. I was also fortunate not to have this common side effect from the surgery. Usually seizures occur within the first 48 hours after surgery and the patient is then medicated for epilepsy. Epilepsy would mean never being able to drive or race a motor vehicle again. As soon as Professor Morgan opened up my skull, he effectively took my car licence away for a time. "How long would it be before I could race a motorcycle again?" Three months, said the professor, and he was prepared to write a letter to help me regain my racing licence from the FIM. After he read it out, I did a quick calculation and realised this would be after the fourth round at Donington in England. "Can you rewrite the letter to make it 12 weeks?" I asked, hopeful of making the grid at Donington. He smiled in agreement.

It almost sounded as if he'd been through this scenario before because he went on: "If you go back too early, it could damage your career." I knew I had no options because, in my contract, there were certain criteria I had to meet, otherwise it could be terminated. So if I rode too early and didn't perform it would be no worse than not riding and losing my job. It was probably bad timing on my part but my current contract had been changed due, I felt, to Mick Doohan's huge career-ending accident. HRC were now covering their asses. I thought HRC would use the contract to the letter as I was already suffering penalties in my pay packet.

My contract with Castrol Honda was due for renewal at the end of 2000. Under the new clause in the contract, if I didn't participate after a specified number of weeks, my payments would stop. Meanwhile the team looked around for a replacement for me. Once again Simon Crafar filled the breach in the team ranks, just like he had for Doug Polen back in 1995. However, Simon hated the Michelin tyres with a passion, and he wasn't such a super substitute. He rode my bikes in the first two rounds of the championship, his performances a total contrast to Colin's. Where Colin gave the VTR1000 SPW its first race win in its very first outing at Kylami, South Africa, Simon struggled to bring my bike home in 14th. In the second race Colin dropped a place to second, and Simon gained one to finish 13th.

At Phillip Island, the changing of the World Superbike guard in the 21st Century took another turn when Carl Fogarty collided with Robert Ulm coming out of southern loop. He broke his upper arm and right shoulder right across the ball joint. The accident marked the end of my rival's WSB career. However, Castrol Honda couldn't capitalise on Ducati's tragedy. The red bikes might now have had only rookie Ben Bostrom riding for the factory team, but Colin collected a pair of fifths, Crafar a DNF and an eighth. I went to Phillip Island to prove to people I was on the road to recovery as phone calls had been my only contact since the operation. This would be the proof. I bleached my hair and went back with an attitude. Phillip Island saw the second replacement rider announced for my bike, and I was sufficiently encouraged by their results to believe I'd be able to step on the bike at round four and not embarrass myself.

At Sugo, my bike was handed over to Manahu Kamada, who HRC must have considered to be a rising young star. He turned out to be a backmarker instead, finishing 16th in the first race, and 15th in the second. Colin just made the top five in the first race, and onto the podium in the second. Watching from afar, it was clear to me the new V-twin had its problems, and I yearned to be racing with the team again to help sort them out.

Before the fourth round at Donington, Megan and I returned to Europe in the hope I'd be granted a licence to race again. This was after one of the longest times I had spent in New Zealand for years. So it was both emotional, as I was leaving my family in full health, and exciting, as I would be continuing with my racing career. Maybe I could have taken the easier option - which would have been part payment - and retired right there and then. If I had won a world championship then maybe the softer option would have been more attractive, but I felt I still had a lot of unfinished business in World Superbike. I now had good reasons why it had been such a slog in '99. The main motivation to get back on the bike was to prove to myself and others I could be my old self by the end of 2000, and hopefully consolidate my position in the team for a crack at the championship in 2001.

We left New Zealand only eight and a half weeks after the operation with positive thoughts that I would be able to ride 12 weeks after the surgery. That time period coincided with Friday morning practice at Donington, England. It was 12 weeks to the day of the operation so I had my argument prepared that, as the UK was nine hours behind Australia, it was really 12 weeks, almost to the hour, as my operation had been at 9p.m. Friday night and practice started at 10.45a.m. Friday.

Before I could concentrate on Donington we had to do some business in Monaco. The Monday following the operation we were meant to have moved apartments. Thanks to some friends, Didier and Kate, along with a lot of help from Sam Davies as well as the agents they boxed everything and moved us. So we unpacked and went out furniture shopping, as our previous apartment had been furnished. At the weekend we sat down and watched the Sugo race. I can remember thinking to myself that Honda or the team hadn't improved the rear traction as I saw Colin sliding all over the place. When I returned to racing one of my first comments was "I could do the testing", to improve the bike in the team's best interests as well as mine for the following year. It never seemed to happen, and in 2001 Colin still struggled with lack of traction and front end feel.

It was great to be back in Monaco but the days became a blur, as there was just too much to do. I was trying to fit in training, organise living, preparing my argument for the FIM and above all, trying to heal.

Eleven weeks after surgery, I flew from Nice to England, collected the motorhome and drove myself straight to Donington. I drove my 40-foot left hand drive bus on the M25 at a time when it was debatable whether I was supposed to be driving a car. I thought racing a superbike would be easy compared to this.

The next week would be full of press engagements plus fitting in all the necessary doctors' appointments demanded by the FIM to regain my licence. I felt it was all too much, way too much, and struggled to keep a brave face. I knew if I showed any weakness, or wanted any special treatment, it would prove I wasn't back to normal.

I was something of a test case for the FIM. No motorcycle racer had made a comeback from brain surgery before. The job of assessing me was handed to Dr Sid Watkins, the Formula One doctor who had given the OK to Mika Hakkinen after he sustained head injuries in his early days with McLaren. Castrol Honda PR officer Chris Herring had arranged a full schedule of PR events in the lead up to these tests. On the Saturday before the race weekend, there was a shop opening, then another one on the Sunday, before an hour- long test at Donington on the Monday. The shop openings were at opposite ends of England, so I borrowed a car from Honda and drove to them.

On Monday I had a one-hour test on the Donington short circuit in front of the FIM doctor. I cut a lap time of 1.11.5 on the short circuit, but this still didn't satisfy him enough to grant me an immediate clearance to race. There were more PR obligations that afternoon, and the following day. I hopped out of my leathers, showered, and drove to Lincoln for another shop opening, and then drove on to Louth to stay the night for the team's open day at the workshop. This went on for four or five hours. While I was there, my father rang to give me the good news that I had been nominated for the New Zealand Order of Merit. So I treated myself to a half hour massage at the Kenwick gym, but at 6p.m. I had to be at the Louth school for another two hours. It was another goodwill thing. Then I drove for two hours back to Donington and the motorhome. It was a hell of a schedule leading to my first race back, and I felt every aspect of being a professional racer was being tested. I couldn't believe what the team was asking and expecting of me, but I was in no position to argue.

On Wednesday I drove back down to London for Dr Watkins' assessment. He gave me a thorough examination, which left me feeling confident about my progress, and him confident about me being able to race again. He advised the FIM accordingly. There was a meeting scheduled with the FIM to confirm Dr Watkins' findings, on the Thursday morning at Donington. The FIM's representatives didn't show up. I was extremely pissed off, as this was my life they were messing with and I had put in so much hard work to try to convince them I was OK. Neil contacted the FIM and we rescheduled for Friday morning.

I attended a press conference that afternoon Chris had set up, but I still couldn't confirm I'd actually be racing that coming Sunday. It wasn't until Friday morning that the FIM finally conducted their "further tests".

I had another hour-long examination with Dr John Firth, who then gave me a temporary clearance to ride in that morning's free practice session, so he could assess me on the bike, and after a ride. I was the first bike out that day, and I wheelied the VTR all the length of the pit straight to the cheers of the fans. It was an emotional return. People kept coming up to me that day, shaking my hand, and saying how glad they were to see me back. When I was asked why I wheelied, my reply was simple – "because I could". After the ride I went straight back to see the doctor, and he finally approved the return of my licence, just in time for the first qualifying session.

It was 12 weeks to the day since I had my operation, so both the doctors I had seen that week covered their backs by following Professor Morgan's recommendation to the letter. Now all eyes were on me as I took the VTR out to qualify. Every one on the track seemed to be giving me extra room, as if they thought my head might explode at any moment, and I'd crash in front of them, and take them out. I was so happy to be on the bike again, I just had to wheelie it everywhere. I was overcome by the sheer joy of riding again.

It was a huge relief to be allowed to race again. It was like the third chance of my career. It had all so nearly been snuffed out by the hand injury at Suzuka in 1990. Now I was being allowed a third chance of becoming a world champion. It was too late in 2000 for such a goal, as I'd already missed three rounds, but I thought that if we could sort out the VTR more, then 2001 might finally be my year. Little did I know that back at HRC in Japan, where a new regime of management was now in control, my comeback to racing was neither being encouraged nor appreciated. I had worked hard to get back on the bike, but in the inner sanctum of the mighty Honda Racing Corporation, my return wasn't being welcomed.

My team was a different story. Every one seemed pleased to have me back on board again. Neil had been totally supportive of all my efforts to get back to racing. I had a new chief mechanic, with Chris Pike replacing Norris. I had always had a great working relationship with Chris, and he had been with the team for some time, as a chassis mechanic then a data analyst. He had a knack of saying the right things at the right time to get me fired up. He'd say it so softly I'd just catch what he said under my helmet as we fired up the bike and headed to the track. The soft way he spoke made me feel the comment was just for me. The VTR had the luxury of an electric starter because the rest of it was so light, Honda could afford the added weight of a starter motor to bring it up to the minimum weight of 162 kgs. So unlike Ducati, we didn't have to use rollers to start the bike, and there was less stress on the transmission when firing it up, when the big fat pistons would have to overcome the high compression.

I was soon putting pressure on myself. It probably was too early to return to racing at this level. The FIM had judged me fit, and I felt I had to get the results immediately to match and justify that judgment. I qualified 13th, and won that grid position in Superpole. Then I finished ninth and seventh in my first races back. I was happy with that. They were big improvements on what my replacements had achieved, and in the second leg I was the first Honda home after Colin crashed. Next day I drove the motorhome all the way down to Monza, Italy. There was still no time to rest. The hard life of chasing the World Superbike series had begun again.

At Monza the following weekend, I crashed during my Superpole lap. It was great to get the first crash out of the way, but I was on target for pole position at the time. It happened in the last turn. I jumped up, bowed to the cheering crowd, and didn't really bother about it too much. I was back! The Monza crowd was typical of every round that year. There were banners welcoming me back everywhere, mobs rushing to see me. I'm sure they all must have thought my racing was over when they heard the reports about my emergency brain surgery. I was being welcomed back like Lazarus.

Then I suddenly developed chest pains, at home one night in Monaco. I couldn't determine their origin. Concerned that it was some side effect from my operation I admitted myself to the Monaco hospital. It was the Tuesday night before Misano race weekend so obviously I had to keep it quiet in case I was deemed unfit to ride. Only Megan and my chief mechanic Chris knew I was wondering whether I could continue to race that season. The doctors, in their very limited English, suggested it could be my heart. It was a scary thought. First my brain, now my heart? After their tests proved negative, I discharged myself the next morning with no answers, and drove to Misano.

Months later while visiting my GP in New Zealand, it was discovered that my neck had been dislodged during the brain surgery. Apparently, this is not uncommon as your head is placed into an odd position and made completely immobile for brain surgery. My neck being out had caused shooting pains through my arm and into my chest, confusing me and the doctors into thinking the chest pains were related to my heart. A quick visit to my chiropractor, and I was back to normal.

I started urging Neil to utilise my track times during the race weekends for testing and developing for 2001, as there was no way I could finish in the top three of the 2000 championship. Not only was I coming in half way through a season, but I had been off the bike for three months, and I'd had brain surgery. So I kept bugging Neil about the weaknesses in the bike. Colin would go on to win eight of the 26 World Superbike races that year, but one weekend he crashed three times, losing the front each time. I told Neil this reflected a lack of feel for the front tyre's traction, and urged him to let me sort it out. But it was hard to get anywhere, as Colin was looking good for the title. Honda obviously felt they were winning, so why change something if it doesn't seem to be broken? They had obviously written me off, because the new parts I wanted were now getting handed on to just one rider - Colin. The new bosses at HRC weren't familiar with my development skills. All the guys who knew me from the RC45 days had been shifted, some to Honda's Formula One programme. Now the people looking after the Superbike development believed there was only one rider worth giving new parts to for the rest of 2000. They might have changed their minds if they'd realised Colin was so focused on winning the title that he didn't have time to test the new bits. He rightly kept his eye on that goal, but behind short-term success there could have been a lot more long-term development going on.

The VTR got such an easy ride in its debut year. Ducati were thrown into total disarray by Fogarty's accident. They had lost their experienced back up riders - Corser and Chili - to Aprilia and Suzuki in 2000. They had tossed them away in favour of a two-rider factory team based around the veteran Fogarty and rookie Bostrom. They were so sure Carl would achieve his stated goal of three-titles-in-a-row that Phillip Island took them by surprise. They were so confused by Fogarty's crash they even tossed away Bostrom mid-season, forcing him into the second tier NCR team. Ben got back at them, though; as soon as Ducati gave him his marching orders, he started performing well. Meanwhile Ducati drafted Aussie Troy Bayliss into the team for Sugo, then suddenly switched to high profile ex-GP star Luca Cadalora for Donington, paying him silly money to ride for them. When Luca took all the lira and ran away and hid at the back of the field, Bayliss got the call once more. By the time Ducati Performance finally settled on its riders, it was too late to stop Colin winning the championship. The factory Ducati team sponsor was Internet company Infostrada. Their paddock nickname became Infodrama. They were a joke in 2000. For proof one only has to look at the performance of the second-tier Ducati teams. Bostrom on the NCR Ducati, and Hodgson on the British INS/GSE bike posed as big a challenge to the factory Honda as the factory bikes ridden by Bayliss and Juan Borja.

The Aprilia was underdeveloped although Corser still gave it several days in the sun, by winning five races. Basically, the Italians were thrown by Honda's trespass into their V-twin engine territory. They had known for years the rules favoured the 1000cc twins over the 750cc fours, and when Honda suddenly played the same game, they just stood back and let the VTR win the title. The only real threat to Colin was Noriyuki Haga in his last year on the Yamaha superbike. The FIM took Noriyuki out of the play by slapping a two-week suspension on him just before the last round at Brands Hatch. They could have easily delayed the ban until after the season to keep interest in the championship alive. Now I don't support any mixing of drugs and racing, but when Haga lost his day in court after a failed drugs test earlier in the year, due to using a dietary supplement, it effectively made Colin a champion by default. I felt a bit sorry for Colin for that. He never got to cross a finish line, flush with the heat of victory.

My appeals for improved parts for the VTR fell on deaf ears, and Honda lost the opportunity of a repeat title in 2001. I should have read more into the development inertia that had infected HRC in 2000. There was obviously a new attitude at Honda's R & D company; one possibly driven by tighter budgets overseen by less experienced managers. I felt my riding improved as the season went on, even if the bike stagnated. In a wet first race and a dry second at Assen, I picked up a fifth and a fourth, and came closer to getting back on the podium. Little did I know, my fate was already sealed back in Japan. Those calling the shots at HRC had obviously expected me to take the soft option and retire. They hadn't counted on my Kiwi grit overcoming what they saw as impossible odds that I'd ever race again.

As the end of the season approached, I'd ask Neil what was happening for next year. He told me HRC were still working it out. Then after the penultimate round at Germany, he said things weren't looking good, and maybe I should start talking to other teams as there were big changes afoot. Evidently the 500 Grand Prix team was going to run just three riders in 2000, and that left Tady Okada without a ride. He also said Honda Motors Europe were going to oversee the Superbike campaign instead of HRC. So I called HME to ask who they'd rather run - Tady or me?

They said I had a higher profile in Europe, therefore I would be their first choice. It lulled me into a false sense of security. I should have known Honda would favour Okada, the rider they saw every day, rather than the one who lived on the other side of the world.

I talked to Davide Tardozzi about joining Ducati. To me, I had all the experience that had been so lacking at Ducati Performance in 2000. A three-rider team of me, Bostrom and Bayliss would have been a force to be reckoned with. Two guys new to World Superbike backed up by a veteran with development skills acknowledged as some of the best in the paddock. It was a dream team, and that's exactly what it stayed - a dream. Tardozzi went and signed Bostrom, Bayliss, and Reuben Xaus for 2001.

The NCR team wanted me to replace Bostrom, but couldn't afford to pay me for the privilege. I contacted Yamaha who, stung by the Haga debacle, were getting out of Superbikes in 2001, and putting all their racing budget into Grand Prix, and its developing four-stroke future. By the last round at Brands Hatch all my options were closing on me. On the Saturday night before the last races of the season, Honda's axe fell.

There was to be a little party that night to celebrate the court decision which handed Colin the championship, but I first got wind of my sacking when one of my mechanics told me he'd signed some sort of presentation plaque for me. At the party, they presented me with an award for seven years of service to Castrol Honda. It was their way of sacking me. It was an award which said, between the lines, there wouldn't be an eighth year with the team. They gave me these two huge plaques with lots of messages written on them. I wasn't prepared for this presentation as, officially, I'd been told no decision had been made about my future in the team.

Colin thanked me for everything he had learned from me - "Dude, it's been fun riding with you, absorbing the experience you have. Good luck + we will see you around. Colin Edwards II." The thought I'd had a couple of years earlier about Adrian taking my technical information and a teammate absorbing my experience had come true! Our Michelin man said I was the best rider he had ever worked with for helping develop their tyres. Mr Flammini said I was the strongest rider he'd ever seen on the brakes, and he hoped I'd race in his series again soon. These were the sorts of things written all over the awards in gold ink. Chris Herring must have scoured the world for those sentiments. There was even one from the departed head of HRC thanking me for my role in developing the RC45. They were all wonderful testimonials to my skill and commitment as a rider, yet they didn't make me feel any better because this was my golden handshake. This was good-bye.

My eyes filled with tears, and I just walked away. I couldn't thank my team or even manage a general thank you to everybody. I just wandered off to be alone, clutching awards covered with reasons why I shouldn't have been sacked, overcome by the painful irony of it all. I was embarrassed with the situation and in shock.

Next day I couldn't wait for the races to end. I couldn't wait to jump off the VTR, rip off all my Castrol Honda gear, and throw it as far as I could into the crowd. I couldn't believe the way Castrol Honda had publicly embarrassed me the night before in front of the press and my colleagues. I wanted to make a statement saying so. After I crossed the line, I made a beeline for the fence. I threw everything into the crowd - boots, gloves, helmet. Finally my leathers. Full of Castrol and Honda logos, these would not join my large collection of leathers back home. Over the fence they flew. The crowd went into a frenzy as people grabbed an arm here, and a leg there, and started a tug of war for the most expensive gift of all. I noticed a young boy in a Castrol Honda sweatshirt. He was about the age I was when I first rode a motorcycle. So I yelled at the crowd to please give the leathers to the boy. They obeyed, calming down, and stepping back to give him room to admire his prize. It was my last act as a rider for Castrol Honda.

twelve

Last of The Mohicans

The way the Brands Hatch crowd suddenly put personal greed aside, and let the boy have the leathers, was a mark of their respect for me. Later, a photo arrived for me of the lad inside the leathers and, strike me if his name wasn't Aaron. Yet respect was sadly lacking on my side of the fence. It has become an increasingly rare commodity in motorsport. Perhaps we should stop calling it a sport at all. Motorbusiness is a more apt description in the 21st Century. The powerful people who determine who rides what, and who drives that, no longer recognise talent as the prime reason for signing someone. Their focus is more on the marketing advantages any particular driver or rider brings to a team. Will they bring extra sponsorship? What sort of profile do they have? Do they suit our image? These are now the most important questions for most team movers and shakers.

Yet one thing endures above all the politics that shape motorsport, and that is the enthusiasm of the fans. My own Slight Advantage fans went ballistic in 1996 when I first started bleaching or colouring my hair, and shaved it into a Mohawk. It was a move inspired by rock music, and I used it to fire me up before a race. Music wasn't just a motivator for me; it was a comfort when times were tough, and a boredom buster through the drudgery of travelling from track to track.

When Carl Fogarty joined Castrol Honda in 1996, I thought why not have a little fun with my appearance? The shock value in the paddock was priceless. Suddenly I was the centre of attention for the media and fans alike. Each weekend I'd change the colour of my hair. It reached a point where I started to run out of colours to use. The fans loved it. There'd be huge queues at the autograph tables wanting my signature. Sales of Arai and, later, Suomy 'Aaron Slight replica' helmets soared. Even the sponsors, whose reaction I'd initially been wary of, loved the way the zany haircuts raised the profile of the team.

Some in the media started calling me "The Last of the Mohicans," as the movie of the James Fenimore Cooper classic was doing the rounds when I first wore a Mohawk. Perhaps "Last of the Chero-Kiwis" was a better description. For I believe I'm the last of the caravan-living, hard-riding motorcycle racers from a little country in the South Pacific, who'll come to Europe in the hope that their raw talent will win them the opportunity of a factory ride.

New Zealand has a proud and long tradition of producing world-class motorcycle racers. There was TT winner Rod Coleman in the '50s, double world champion Hugh Anderson in the '60s, Ivan Mauger's unequalled record of world speedway crowns, Shayne King's 1996 World 500cc Motocross crown, and a whole host of World 500cc Grand Prix runners-up - Kim Newcombe, Ginger Molloy, Keith Turner, and Graeme Crosby. All of these guys squeezed their success out of an increasingly barren motorcycle racing world. A world where nationality is becoming increasingly more important than talent, means it's unlikely there'll be any young Kiwi racers able to follow in our footsteps. Track owners' recordings of the New Zealand national anthem will gather dust from now on, because no New Zealanders will be able to break into a factory ride. The walls surrounding the corporate camps have just got too high to scale on talent alone, and their gates are open to riders of nations where there are high volumes of motorcycles sold, or riders can bring the big corporate sponsors. Marketing is the tail that now wags the dog in the motorcycle racing world.

My haircuts helped break down those barriers. People of all nations could relate to the celebration of individual expression they represented. The bottom line is that it doesn't matter where you're from, or what you look like, it's how you relate to people that really counts. All I felt from the fans throughout my career was total respect. Through most of the 1990s I was the man on the 750cc underdog most likely to upset the Ducati applecart. People could relate that position to their own lives, their own personal battles in business or their career, and take inspiration from it. When I picked up the bike again at Nurburgring in 1998, and crossed the line in fourth to the biggest cheer of the day, the crowd responded because they could relate to what that action represented in their own lives. It was something that said it doesn't matter how bruised and battered you are from the knock backs in life, you can pick yourself up, dust yourself down and fight on.

I have taken pride in not being too different from the young man who left Masterton, New Zealand all those years ago to chase a dream. My success has not clouded or changed my view of life. I return to New Zealand and enjoy the slow, relaxed way of life just as much as I enjoy my new lifestyle and friends, endless summers and financial success. I still race to win and to fulfil my own personal ambition and passion for speed, not to please the money-makers or to make more money. I have battled along the way and sacrificed plenty, mostly on a personal level, as there was only room for one major goal in my life - the World Superbike championship. Unfortunately I never took the title but will never feel less for it. The experiences are countless and the lessons learned invaluable. Through it all the most constant encouragement and inspiration came from my fans, and they made up for all the times I felt a long way from family and friends.

Whenever I saw a rider wearing one of my replica helmets, or a bike painted up to look like my racebike, it filled me with pride to the point of putting a lump in my throat. Anytime I felt racing was getting me down, it was the fans who lifted me up again. One was Zoe, who always sent me a huge hand-made card before a race. We'd put Zoe's cards on display in the motorhome to see every day during the race weekend. It was my own personal inspiration. Sometimes the card wouldn't arrive in time for the weekend because of a mail glitch. Next weekend there would be two of Zoe's cards. They always said the same thing in different ways - "thinking of you, and wishing you every success this weekend". Then there was the Austrian baker who sent his well-wishing messages in the most delicious edible forms. He'd shape his baking into my number, one of my helmet designs, or a replica of the New Zealand flag. We eagerly took these messages of support on board. At Easter, there would be gifts of eggs from nearly everyone looking for an autograph. There would be knocks on our door to exchange the gifts, a signature for an egg. I think the fans realised Megan and I were going without the little touches that make a place home and during all the years the fans were our adopted family. Where most people have day-to-day contact with their family, we had my fans. Our exchanges weren't limited by circuit fences. I would be stopped grocery shopping in England, or walking around the port of Monaco. Children are my weakness, and their enthusiasm I believe worth whatever time and effort I can give them. A simple signature gained in childhood can turn into a life long dream to follow. Children learn quickly and you never know, it could be a pivotal moment in their lives, changing them forever.

Another constant in my life has been my personal sponsors. To begin with they were Japanese based companies when I first arrived in Europe - Arai helmets and Kushitani leathers, boots and gloves. Arai were a long lasting relationship which began with the purchase of my first ever road race helmet, which saved me in that head on crash with the Morris coming through Featherston years earlier in New Zealand. As my profile grew and sponsorship was offered, I easily accepted the deal from Arai. This partnership saw the design and sale of replica helmets. It was a business deal all the same and, when the contracts started to become difficult for Arai to commit to, I found a new sponsor who was completely committed to my racing and me. With my new Italian helmet sponsor - Suomy - I added another Italian sponsor to my list.

Previously I had entered into a contract with Sidi boots and Spyke leathers. I signed these contracts because they were family companies and seemed to be appreciative of my efforts and welcomed us into their families. The Italians with their open arms and hearts soon became our friends. It was easy doing business with people who cared.

Lots of support came from New Zealand as well. In 1998, I received a Maori bone carving from Piki, an old mate I used to play basketball with back in Masterton. It had the number '111' carved into the overall design, and he suggested I wear it around my neck for luck. As the season played out, I began to wonder whether a tohunga (priest) had blessed it first or not. Then again, maybe my luck would have been even worse if I hadn't been wearing Piki's carving. One day I was walking down a Wellington street and a man came up to me and asked me to wait for just a moment. He had a gift for me. He proudly came back with the most magnificent ornately carved wooden Maori club (mere) from a display shelf in his shop and presented me with it, wishing me luck. This has been with us in the motorhome ever since, and gets taken to the bedside table every night just in case we needed protection during the long hauls and sleeping on the side of the road.

The local Masterton radio station, 89FM, once wrote a song about me, and played it over and over again anytime I raced on the other side of the world. This was the year my race bike was seen hooning down the streets of Masterton in front of my hometown crowd. The mayor of the town appointed me Masterton's official ambassador to the world, and we had a party at Burridges to celebrate. The song 89FM had written was played endlessly. We danced the night away to it.

Carl Fogarty and I could have compared awards had the New Zealand honours system not moved away from the Queen. I was awarded the new, more republican equivalent - Member of the New Zealand Order of Merit for my contribution to motorcycling. One day soon I'll drop into Government House in Wellington for the official presentation ceremony. I've been busy elsewhere on ceremony dates so far.

In the early years of World Superbike, it was one big happy family and everyone got together on a Sunday night and enjoyed the tales of the weekend, happy for whoever had won. As the sport grew so did the money, the pressure and the political wheeling and dealing. The teams became more sponsor orientated, so there was more pressure put on everybody. Team numbers grew, hospitality suites started to appear and promotion got bigger every year. Riders were expected to participate in dinners and other PR events to please the sponsors, even if it was on a Saturday night prior to the big race day.

Flammini failed to realise the pressures mounting on riders and still wanted to keep the World Superbike paddock open to the public and the riders accessible. This became increasingly difficult over the years and added even more pressure and stress when there had to be crowd control and security just so we could get on with the job. The days of simply chucking your leathers on and racing to win quickly disappeared. There were other priorities as far as teams and their sponsors were concerned. Money began to talk. Riders had to focus on always smiling and pleasing the money makers/suppliers, while keeping their performance sharp. It became more difficult to keep the relaxed paddock atmosphere that World Superbike was famous for, and the Flammini Group was trying to retain. They correctly identified that it was this atmosphere which helped the code to grow at a time when attendances at Grand Prix were in decline. However, World Superbike didn't seem to want to learn from the mistakes of the Ecclestone-led Grand Prix series. It quickly grew into a GP-like world, and now that Grand Prix motorcycle racing is moving to a Formula One-like four-stroke formula, World Superbike faces its biggest challenge yet.

My personal thoughts on the changes ahead are merely educated guesses. The 2001 World Superbike season produced some of the best racing I have seen. Why? Because there were eight V-twin 1000s at the front. This really speaks for itself as everybody had the same rule restrictions to work with. The guys on the 750s couldn't be seen, as they definitely got less performance from their machines. Given the rule restrictions, I see the remainder of the Japanese four cylinder bikes pulling out in the near future, as they're getting beaten badly by a lot more V-twins on the track. For me the advantage of the twins has been obvious for many years. It now looks worse as there are more V-twins competing at the front of the field. I see the new GP1 formula for the Grand Prix heading down the same rocky road. Why do the FIM want to have complicated rules that place displacement and weight handicaps on certain engine formats? This makes it hard to create a level playing field, and I am sure they have no technical evidence that the formulas they introduce will create equal and close racing. Even during the last decade 500 riders used to complain about the speed of the NSR500 Honda. At least it was a 500cc V4 two-stroke just like their Suzuki or Yamaha. Grand Prix racing is about to make the same mistake as World Superbike, favouring one engine format over another by giving it a displacement break. There will also be different weights for different configurations. Three cylinder machines will carry less weight than four cylinder and so on. Another limiting factor will be regulations on four stroke fuel tank capacities. All too complicated and confusing for me, let alone the fans in the stands. If it produces great racing, I will be happy to be proved wrong.

In the early Superbike days there were only a few caravans in the paddock, and a lot of the teams used their semi-trailers as accommodation and kitchens as well as bike transporters and workshops. The Bertocchi Kawasaki team were in one of the trailers. They are still around today and we have remained friends ever since. Sergio and Mariolina immediately welcomed the Kiwis in their midst and introduced us to black espresso and their great tiramisu. Their mechanics also instantly accepted us foreigners and it meant a lot, as we were new to Europe and the World Superbike championship. We had a lot of laughs with 'Arnie', who we met through the Bertocchis. Albert was his real name, but he reminded us of Arnold Schwarzenegger. Arnie was always one of the keenest participants in the drinking games.

One took place at the pub on the hill at the A1-ring, which was famous for its view over the Austrian circuit. After a mixed result - a second and an engine blow-up - we took to the hill for some celebrating and commiserating. My father and his partner Janis were with us, and we joined the rest of the paddock at the pub for some R&R. Arnie joined the party later in the night just after I had smoked 'Slick' Bass in a drinking race. Slick could always sniff out a decent do. When Arnie walked in I bet him I could get up on top of the door with no aid. Which I immediately did. Arnie, with his huge physique, tried to follow. The door had a glass pane, and it was not necessarily the right door for such a game, but we'd had a few. As he swung up, imitating my method, he went through the glass. After shattering the door, the party was quickly called off. We all had to put our hands in our pockets for the repairs.

Belgarda Yamaha, another team which was there at the beginning, is still competing today. Davide Brivio, team manager, and Maio Meregali, who raced for Belgarda, are friends still. The team has undergone many changes over the years and Davide was always trying to secure my services as a Superbike rider. Today Maio is team manager of Belgarda Yamaha, which only competes in the Supersport championship. Unlike the early days, where they only ran Fabrizio Pirovano on a superbike.

Fabri is fast and smooth, especially in the wet. He is a man after my own heart, and he would always have the cleanest motorhome in the paddock. We communicate with Fabri through his partner Sylvie as he has never taken to the English language and we have been a bit slack not to have learned Italian. It never stood in the way; there were, after all, always hand signals. Fabri is proud and a total perfectionist, small in stature but the biggest kid at heart.

Giancarlo Falappa had a strong presence in the paddock and a very powerful personality. The Fogarty children were terrified of the big Italian when Giancarlo and Carl were teammates. Although Falappa came across as a big imposing hulk, he was always very friendly once you got to know him. Unfortunately his accident left him with some physical limits that cut his riding career short, but he still takes his motorhome to meetings, and remains part of the World Superbike scene.

Jeffry De Vries and his girlfriend (now wife), Bianca, were there from the beginning, with their sponsor's trailer, from Holland. They would bring many of their friends along as mechanics and, because they spoke English, we became very close and still try to visit them anytime the racing takes us to Assen.

Scott Russell was always good entertainment because he had such Euro-shock whenever he came to race World Superbike. He had to follow us on the autobahns and autoroutes because he couldn't believe the toll booth operators wouldn't accept American dollars. We'd pay Scott's passage for him; otherwise he might not have got to the racetrack on time. He had an attention span of seconds. He once invited Megan and me over to his motorhome to watch a video. After 20 minutes watching the movie, we noticed Scott had disappeared. He was outside, pulling wheelies on his mountain bike. He had gotten bored with the video.

Troy Corser and his buddy Jim Beam were always close and you could be certain they would attend every party going. The arrival of the young Australians in the mid-1990s bought a new party-boy era to the paddock. Troy and Anthony Gobert were always looking for something to do on a Sunday night, Monday night, Tuesday night, Wednesday night. Any night when there wasn't important business to settle the next day. The parties became legendary and were sometimes a distraction I had to avoid. I had to sort out young Anthony out several times, once when he kept banging on the door of our motorhome, trying to invite me outside to have a drink with him and his mates. He just wouldn't take no for an answer. He was a hugely talented rider, and could have achieved a lot more if he had backed up that raw talent with work and commitment.

He was later to be the first guy to fail a random drug test. We were not surprised, and in some ways relieved, as it was dangerous on the track and we thought he would be penalised with some kind of ban. Disappointingly, the AMA didn't take a stand and Anthony was reissued with a licence to race in America. Rumours were that he was still not clean and that he had failed more than one drug test. The FIM didn't approve his licence to enter into the Laguna Seca round of the World Superbike race. However, they did not follow this any further. So racing in America resumed, after Anthony, to clear himself, submitted more tests. There was no international ban. How could a controlling body like the FIM not take action against such dangerous and irresponsible, definitely illegal behaviour?

Ducati had a press conference at Laguna to try to smooth the way and explain why Anthony was not riding in the World Superbike race at Laguna. The question was asked, "Would the three Ducati team managers take him back to ride in Europe?" They said yes, as he was just too fast! I stood up at the back of the room then and said, "So is Ben Johnson, and do you see him still running?"

We were always glad to see Jamie Whitham - the great English funny man with a story for every occasion. He has an excellent sense of humour and is always great company. He was a huge inspiration to me in the way he dealt with his cancer scare and came back as strong on the track.

Jamie also plays drums in a band - ' The Po Boys'. They are frequent entertainers of the paddock, putting on great parties and rock music. Jamie has the perfect partner in wife Andrea, whose sense of fun easily matches his.

Since the early days mentioned above, these friendships, along with others, have kept us grounded and added fun into our often stressful life. Even though many are not mentioned specifically, it is like a Japanese photographer once said to me - "You don't take photos of the firework display, you remember it in your heart." And motorsport isn't the only industry where I have made good friends. Despite our different professions, success in our respective fields and living in the public eye has given us some common ground.

My Superbike 'family' was a hard one to leave, but in 2001 I tried to pursue a career racing on four wheels. Car racing is something I've dallied with at times. It started with racing a Toyota Corolla with Ross Meekings, in the Wellington street race held on the city's harbourside, which used to be a round in the now defunct Pan-Pacific Touring Car Championship. We took the little Corolla to third in its class in the endurance race that many called the "Monaco of the South Pacific" for its café-side atmosphere. Then in 1994, I leased a Formula Ford single-seater and found time for three rounds of the New Zealand Formula Ford Championship. My first race was at the Wellington circuit around the waterfront where I was taken out in the first corner. Pukekohe followed and I had two fourths, after very tight racing. The third round was cancelled because of rain but I had managed to dice with Kenny Smith, a multi-time New Zealand Grand Prix winner, Jason Richards, New Zealand

Touring Car Champ, and New Zealand TraNZam champion Ashley Stichbury. Then in 1997 Chris Herring jacked me up a drive in the British Touring Car Championship at Donington. I turned up expecting some little Civic to race in a support class, but found it was Tarquini's 'full monty' works Accord in the main events. I qualified seventh in a field of 22 factory cars. It was a pity the rest of the race didn't live up to the promise of qualifying. Yvan Muller tapped me in the rear three-quarter panel with the works Audi, and I smacked into the wall going down the Craner Curves backwards.

In 2001, I had a similar race with the Peugeot team in the BTCC. I showed some promise, leading the race at one stage, then the contact nature of saloon car racing bit me again. Another tap in the back, then a shunt in the front, left me limping back to the pits. Peugeot were keen for me to keep on racing for them, but I needed to find more sponsorship to get them to run another car for me full-time. Then I got a third racing in the ASCAR Mintex Cup race that supported the CART event at the newly formed Rockingham Oval. They positioned me 11th on the grid as there had been no qualifying due to conditions. During the race I progressed up the field finishing third. On the way I overtook sportscar aces Neil Cunningham and Mark Proctor. I impressed the team owner enough in this specialised event to be offered a more permanent drive.

I am the rider who has ridden in the most World Superbike races, with 229 starts. I've recorded 18 fastest laps in races, secured eight pole positions, and stood on the podium a total of 87 times. Of all the other riders in the history of World Superbike, only Carl Fogarty has been up there more times than me.